SEAN CONWAY'S
CULTIVATING
LIFE

SEAN CONWAY'S
CULTIVATING
LIFE

SEAN CONWAY
LEE ALAN BUTTALA

ARTISAN

FRONTISPIECE: Inspired reuse of simple, inexpensive material turns this snow fencing into a more permanent enclosure. By setting readily available lath snow fencing into a simple cedar framework, friends have taken an ordinary material and given it the magic of a Japanese bamboo fence.

OPPOSITE: While early-flowering daffodils are a sure harbinger of spring, purple snake's head fritillaria, yellow trout lilies, and Siberian squill are other bulbs worth planting when plotting out a spring garden.

Published by Artisan
A Division of Workman Publishing Company, Inc.
225 Varick Street
New York, NY 10014-4381
www.artisanbooks.com

Library of Congress Cataloging-in-Publication Data

Conway, Sean (Sean J.), 1959–
Sean Conway's cultivating life / Sean Conway and Lee Alan Buttala.
    p. cm.
ISBN 978-1-57965-333-0 — ISBN 978-1-57965-382-8 (pbk.)

1. Garden ornaments and furniture. 2. Gardening. I. Buttala, Lee Alan. II. Title.
III. Title: Cultivating life. IV. Title: 125 projects for backyard living.

SB473.5.C665 2009
635—dc22
2008022244

Design by Stephanie Huntwork
Illustrations by Liz Pepperell

Printed in China
First printing, February 2009

10 9 8 7 6 5 4 3 2 1

contents

PREFACE: CULTIVATING LIFE, AMERICAN STYLE ix
INTRODUCTION xvi

FERNS, MUSHROOMS, AND MOSS

Fern Stand 2 • Fiddlehead Fern Salad 3 • Creating a Green
Roof for a Shed 5 • Fern Vase 7 • Propagating Ferns 8
Fern under Glass 10 • Mossy Pots 11 • Planting a Wardian
Case 13 • Tropical Moss Jars 15 • Moss Shadow Box 16
Mushroom Print Plates 19

VEGETABLES

Bean Towers 22 • Bean Curry with Cauliflower 24
CSAs: Eating Local and Organic 25 • Bean Trellis 26
Bean Votives 29 • Portable Salad Table 30 • Building a Salad
Table 31 • Planting a Salad Table 31 • Cold Frame 33 • Into
the Woods: Getting Comfortable Building Your Own Projects 35
Cedar Potting Bench 37 • Planting Perennial Vegetables 40

OUTDOOR KITCHEN

Outdoor Kitchen 44 • Barbecue Trug 47 • Oak Utensil
Caddy 49 • Chicken Wire Armoire 51 • Sun Prints 53
Bamboo Place Mats 54 • Milk Bottle Bar 55

TOMATOES, CORN, AND PEPPERS

Tomato A-Frames 59 • Pine Nut–Crusted Tomatoes 61
Saving Heirloom Tomato Seed 62 • Hanging Kitchen
Garden 64 • Corn Printing 65 • Corncrib Storage 67
Cornhusk Labels 71 • Chile Ristras and Freezing, Drying,
and Storing Peppers 72 • Making Chile Ristras 72 • Oven
Drying 73 • Roasting and Freezing Peppers 73

HERBS

Cast-Iron Hanging Herb Garden 76 • Backdoor Herb Pot 77
Herb Rail Planter 79 • Drying and Storing Herbs 81

STONE

Stone Tree Marker 84 • Slate-Topped Side Table 86 • Pebble
Mosaic Pots 89 • Hypertufa Troughs 92 • Planting Troughs
with Dwarf Conifers 92 • Hypertufa Nursery Pots 93 • Large
Hypertufa Troughs 94 • Stone Edging 95

FLORA

Lath Bench for Houseplants and Orchids 98
Mounting Miniature Orchids 101 • Cedar Orchid Box 102
Rose Cuttings 104 • Propagating Begonias 105
Climbing Rose Trellis 107 • Agaves with Glass Mulch 109
Bamboo Trellis 110 • Herbarium Specimens 112
Poison Ivy Prints 114 • Tillandsia Mobile 116

FRUIT

Feta Cheese and Watermelon Salad with Raspberry
Vinaigrette 120 • Small-Batch Preserves 120
Orangery Planter 123 • Growing Citrus in Containers 125

GRAINS AND SEEDS

Raised Seedbed 128 • Storing Seeds 128 • Seed Packet
Cork Frame 129 • Mustard from Seed 130 • English Beer
Mustard 131 • Grainy White Wine and Honey Herb Mustard 131
Growing Microgreens 134 • Growing Sprouts 135 • Tabletop
Rice Paddy 137 • Making Rice Paper 138 • Rice Paper Votives 139

FAUNA

Sunflower Seed Bird Feeder 142 • Saltbox Birdhouse 144
Building an Owl House 146 • Butterfly Plants 150
Butterfly Observation Cage 151 • Butterfly Pillow 153
Mushroom Wood Bat House 154

HOME

Setting Up and Customizing a Doghouse 158
Children's Porch Swing 161 • Iron Fence Table 163
Screen Door Curtain 164 • Stock Shed 167 • Pine Bench 168
Milk-Painted Stools 170 • Milk Glass Luminarias 171
Clothesline Trellis 173 • Stilted Hedge Topiary 175
Fixing Terra-cotta Pots 176 • Terra-cotta Chimney Pot 177

WATER

Containerized Water Gardens 180 • Bog Container
Garden 183 • Using a Birdbath for Marginals 184
Water-Gilding a Lily Pad Table 185 • Rain Lilies 187
Rain Barrel 188 • Rain Gauge 189 • Faucet Handle
Coatrack 190 • Bamboo Fountain 192

BULBS

Outdoor Forcing 196 • Drying, Curing, and Braiding
Garlic and Onions 198 • Onion Basket Planter 201
Storing Dahlias 202 • Onionskin Eggs 203

HARVEST

Planting a Belgian Fence 206 • Orchard Ladder
Plant Stand 209 • Weed Basket 211 • Apple Basket
Lamp 212 • Lightbulb Strings 215 • Gourd Lamp 216
Drilling Squash 218 • Curing Heirloom Pumpkins and
Seed Saving 220 • Pumpkin and Cauliflower Gratin 221

TREES

Siting a Tree 224 • Willow Water for Rooting 225
Sculptural Willow Lamp 226 • Land Art Woodpile 229
Maple Syrup Bucket Storage 230 • Maple Scones 231
Oak Storage Box 232 • Japanese Maples in Containers 234
Leaf Sculpture 235 • Compost Bin 236 • Planting and Pruning
a Copper Beech Hedge 240 • Pruning Hornbeams 241

ACKNOWLEDGMENTS 243
RESOURCES 247
INDEX 248

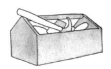

building or crafting

gardening

food and drink

cultivating life,
american style

Every American has his or her own story about turning a house into a home. For some of us, creating a home has meant a very literal return to our roots and to family. For others, the act has required a little more resourcefulness—we need to establish homes where our jobs and spouses take us. But whether we are setting up house in a small Rhode Island town where we grew up (as I did) or building a new life hundreds or even thousands of miles away from family or friends, our sense of home is based in the familiar and the comfortable. From the landscape and trees of our childhoods to the traditions and foods of our hometowns, we return to our roots to develop our home base.

Often defined by our own childhoods in sleepy suburbs, bustling ports, or farm towns, the idea of home is larger than we are. A connection to the American landscape is steeped in the traditions and values that were brought to this country by our forebears, no matter how many generations have passed since they came ashore. In my own case, I am the great-grandson of Irish immigrants, and though I have been influenced by their efforts and choices, I am also greatly influenced by some of Thomas Jefferson's ideas. Jefferson's attempt to live off the land—his efforts to grow his own grapes, raise his own animals, herald the virtues of the tomato (the most American of vegetables), create his own gardens, design outbuildings for smoking meats, and chronicle his horticultural experiments in the garden—defined an American way of life. It is a life that is attached to the seasons and the land as much as to the community around us. And our nation's agrarian roots are not as far behind us as they may seem; in fact, many agricultural practices used in the eighteenth and nineteenth centuries are still employed today, and with the increase in organic farming, they are more in vogue than ever.

But, of course, like Jefferson we are often diverted from these ideals by the hustle and bustle of everyday life and the need to make a living, and my story

Trilliums are as noted for their silver-mottled foliage as for their colorful blooms, and over time will form a nice patch.

is no exception. When I received my bachelor's degree in biology from Fordham University in New York City in 1982, like countless other recent graduates, I had no idea what I wanted to do. In my last semester, I met a graduate student in an animal behavior course at the Bronx Zoo who had done research on migratory raptors in the Midwest. He put me in touch with that program's director. Within weeks of graduation and much to my surprise, I found myself banding migrating hawks, falcons, and the occasional owl at the Cedar Grove Ornithological Station in Cedar Grove, Wisconsin. The station lacked electricity and running water, and the only form of heat was a small wood-burning stove that was lit every morning to stave off the formidable Wisconsin chill. The work was interesting and the natural world around me was inspiring. Summer passed into fall and by the end of October the migration ended and so did my job.

I thought about coming home to Rhode Island or heading west to California to seek my fortune, but in the odd way that opportunity often presents itself, I found myself taking a job in nearby Plymouth, Wisconsin, as a child care counselor in a residential treatment center. I fell in love with the rural nature of Wisconsin and with the friendly residents of this small town. After years of living in New York with my nose to the grindstone, I found the simple life of this town and the friendliness of its inhabitants to be just what I was looking for. Following my first subzero winter, I moved out of the small apartment I had rented and into a farmhouse in the small town of Glen Beulah, Wisconsin. Renting a house instead of an apartment allowed me to create a garden and connect to the surrounding landscape, and would lay the groundwork for changes that were to come in my life.

The farmhouse had belonged for generations to a family named Luth; it was in fact filled with the spirit of these hardworking people. With its old-fashioned General Electric refrigerator topped by a cylindrical cooling element and its ancient washing machine in the basement, which required manual feeding of the clothes through its two red rubber ringers, it was a step back in time. Hanging the laundry out to dry in the sun (or in the basement once winter struck) provided a simple connection to the world around me.

Old Farmer Luth, who had lived on the property all his life, taught me dozens of interesting lessons without my ever having had the opportunity to meet him (he had passed on at the ripe old age of ninety several years before I arrived). Farmer Luth had penciled in the dates of the return of the barn swallows in the hayloft every year. For more than six decades, the birds returned to their nest every year within a week of the same date, showing me the regularity of nature.

His chronicles on the walls of the basement recorded the date of the appearance of the first asparagus every spring. To my surprise, the asparagus, like the barn swallows, followed a regular cycle and, with the aid of Farmer Luth's notes, I began to understand the rhythm of the seasons—and my own attachment to them and to the surrounding world.

Whether it was simply the result of the long Wisconsin winter nights or Farmer Luth's asparagus notes, I began to long for a vegetable garden. In those days, even in the summer, a trip to the grocery store did not offer the array of produce we have available today. In February I was longing for tomatoes that were red and juicy, not white and crunchy, or for some noniceberg lettuce that had an occasional hint of a color other than white. I borrowed some seed catalogs from a friend and within days had put together a seed order that totaled more than $300—more than my rent and beyond my budget. I was forced to scale back (to this day I still find it necessary to curb my annual seed order enthusiasm). That first year, it hadn't even occurred to me that I needed space to start seedlings as well as a cleared and prepared plot of land in which to set them out once they had grown on. I also had no idea how much time it would take to care for even a small garden.

Surprisingly, my first vegetable garden turned out to be a success. The weather was perfect that season, and all summer long I gorged myself on the bounty of my garden. An abundance of peas, zucchini, peppers, tomatoes, squash, and onions provided me with a simple, satisfying diet, and the inheritance from Farmer Luth of an established asparagus bed and a mature raspberry patch provided me with the benefits of a perennial harvest as well. Once I had produced enough overstock to share with my neighbors and coworkers (who in turn shared theirs with me), I was hooked. And before I knew it, my neighbors were teaching me how to can and preserve my bounty so that during the long Wisconsin winter ahead I could have something to enjoy other than the dreaded iceburg lettuce and a few notes about asparagus scribbled on the wall. Gardening still provides me with this sense of community, and I find it to be one of the best ways to connect with neighbors, friends, and family.

As my passion for gardening grew, I decided it was time to leave and pursue my interest in plants and gardening. At about this time, a friend from college who had gone on to study architecture sent me a brochure about a landscape architecture program in Rhode Island. I decided to move back there and take some courses in landscape design. It was hard to leave the farmhouse and garden in Wisconsin, but I was excited about finding a job working in a small garden center in Little Compton, Rhode Island, enabling me to return East. I soon found myself renting a house there and taking a few drafting courses at the University of Rhode Island, where I learned how to measure, use scales, and draw in perspective. One day, while on a class outing to examine the sites of some early Colonial homes, we drove by the residence of the professor of my principles of landscape design course. I was taken aback when he told us he had lived there for twelve years. The "landscape" surrounding his house was nothing more than an endless lawn—there weren't any foundation plantings or any gardens for that matter, not even a single tree. Highway tollbooths had more landscaping than this house. Even worse was the fact that he had pointed his house out to us proudly. I quickly decided that if I was going to learn anything about landscape design, it wasn't going to be in this course, or from this professor.

On the other hand, in my work at the garden center I was learning at an incredible rate. Perennial gardens were just gaining a foothold in this country, and though the nursery where I was working still focused more on annual petunias, impatiens, and marigolds, we were starting to grow interesting perennials. What limited varieties were brought in from wholesale growers in Rhode Island could not meet the growing demand. During this time I was learning how to care for the ever-increasing array of perennials that was becoming available. I familiarized myself with the range of these exciting offerings and how to get the most out of them, and I realized that for me the best method of learning about gardening and plants takes place not in the classroom but by examining the environment where they thrive. I also discovered that this form of education involved "teachers" as well. I learned as much about plants and garden design from the nursery's customers as I did from its owners and the wholesale growers. Even my professor's grass landscape provided an education—albeit in teaching me what not to do.

More than two decades have passed since my move back to Rhode Island. In that time, I have started a landscape design business and founded a nursery noted for its selection of rare and undercultivated annuals, perennials, shrubs, and small trees. (I have since discovered that even common annuals have a role in the garden, and I fill in the empty spaces in my borders with different varieties of colorful annuals each year. I guess plants come in and out of vogue like fashion, which explains our current passion for heirloom varieties of flowers.) More important, I have settled into a wonderful 200-year-old shingled house with my wife, Liz, and our children, Emmett and Fiona, in Tiverton, Rhode Island, where I've learned to nurture more than just plants. In the past few years I've had the good fortune to host *Cultivating Life,* a television series that has taken me across the country in celebration of agrarian, gardening, and building traditions, expanding my sense of community to the nation's borders and allowing me to incorporate great ideas from around the country into my own homestead.

As we take on projects around our house (there's always something to be done, as one look at Liz's patient face tells me), I am always searching for advice. Whether I am working in the gardens, redesigning the terrace, or framing a new chicken coop or duck house (yes, even animals of the domesticated variety have moved in), I often think of heading to the cellar in the vain hope that Farmer Luth has scribbled down the answers to my current home crisis on the wall next to the old washing machine. And though my trips down the cellar steps are often in vain, a few steps across the street to the local metalsmith, a trip to the lumberyard, and even the e-mail advice from an old contractor friend two thousand miles away provide me with the answers to questions of how to move forward with my various projects.

By simply observing and noting our relationship to the world around us, I think we can all learn from people like Jefferson and Farmer Luth. Henry David Thoreau is another great source of wisdom. With his writing and in his life, Thoreau set the stage for us to connect to the cycles and seasons of life and gave it a distinctly American sensibility. Whether the result of our labor is Thoreau's *Walden,* Jefferson's oft-cited studies on varieties of his beloved peas and his success with them in his garden at Monticello, or Farmer Luth's scribblings on the wall, our connection to the land is passed along from generation to generation, taking us far into the past and, with any luck, well into the future.

With this book, I hope that I can take on the role of old Farmer Luth and provide some advice and inspiration for you, whether you are trying to grow vegetables organically, attract birds to your backyard, or create an outdoor kitchen that will become the cornerstone of your family's memories. I don't have any pretensions to being Jefferson or Thoreau, but I like the idea of sharing some of the ideas I have learned along the way with my neighbors across the country — and, in the process, seeing others reconnect with the land as I have.

SEAN CONWAY

Sometimes a familiar flower in an unexpected color turns an old standard into a new favorite. Pink-and-orange cupped daffodils bring a whole new color range to a familiar genus, and make a sole yellow bloom seem extraordinary too.

introduction

Have our backyards become the new great room? As we started to develop *Cultivating Life*, the television series and this companion book, we saw ourselves as two plantsmen: one gardening in New York, Connecticut, and Virginia, the other in Rhode Island. But as we began to examine our lives—and those of our friends, clients, and coworkers—we realized that the backyard had taken on a new role in all of our lives. It is no longer just a patch of grass for impromptu softball and badminton games (that we dread mowing each week) and a tiny patch of vegetables. Instead it is a significant part of our lives. For many months out of the year—and year-round for those of us in even-tempered climates—it is our kitchen, our family room, and a place to entertain friends and family or to find peace and quiet. With the return of the reel mower, it can even replace a morning at the gym (turning cutting the lawn into a moral victory against the battle of the bulge). Even our friends in urban areas were in on the act—converting their brownstone rooftops into orchards and wildlife sanctuaries and transforming patios, balconies, and even fire escapes into containerized vegetable and perennial gardens.

We soon realized that we were no longer talking about creating a simple book about gardening filled with the usual advice on perennials and annuals and how to prepare your vegetable bed. Instead we were creating a primer on how to live more and more of one's life outdoors. But if that is where we are headed as a society, why haven't we reinvented the backyard in the same way we have demanded that our houses meet our modern needs?

The answer is that we have, but we haven't realized it. With the development of grills with infrared side burners and the installation of an outdoor sink and countertop, making dinner outdoors has evolved beyond throwing some hamburgers on the grill and calling everyone to the picnic table. We make cedar-planked salmon, Mexican grilled corn with Cotija cheese, and spaghetti with heirloom tomatoes and basil. Sometimes we even eat off real plates stored conveniently near our outdoor dining space in an open-air hutch made from a stock piece of unpainted furniture. One slightly obsessive friend in Brooklyn even attempts to grow grapes up the back side of his row house so that he can serve local wine with the vegetables he grows a few blocks away in a community plot. By all means, don't ask for a gin and tonic without checking to see if his bathtub is clean.

Wireless servers allow us to bring work home from the office and not be cooped up inside on a beautiful Saturday. Now we catch a few rays of sun while we review, from a comfortable chair on the terrace, marketing reports and e-mail on our laptops. And with any luck we leave some of that work untouched, weed our perennial border instead, and delay facing the state of our business until Monday morning.

We build kitchen gardens that allow us to harvest our own meals—and for those with limited space, we look back to the Hanging Gardens of Babylon in an effort to make room for a litany of herbs and our favorite heirloom tomatoes. Whereas we used to simply reach for the produce labeled "organic" in the grocery store, we now frequent local farmstands for seasonal produce and plant a berry patch out back so that we can harvest a few of our own blueberries to add to our morning cereal.

While we have become more hurried and harried, in the true American spirit, we continually search for ways of improving the quality of our lives. It is as easy as turning off the television, getting beyond our fears of building something for ourselves (see "Into the Woods," page 35), or letting a few e-mails wait until Monday and stepping into our own backyards. It involves making the decision to take an active role in our lives—whether by building and converting a stock shed in our backyard into an outdoor family room (at a fraction of the cost of adding on to our home) or by planting a bed of perennial vegetables, such as asparagus, that we will enjoy from year to year.

One thing is clear. Whether the project we take on is large (for instance, a hypertufa trough for growing succulents or dwarf conifers) or small (converting an old tool bin into a barbecue trug), we can simplify our lives and make outdoor living easier, and in the process we can find time to reconnect with family and friends and our own need to create and have pride in the work we do.

FERNS, MUSHROOMS, AND MOSS

The unfurling fronds of ferns have come to symbolize the beginning of spring. The architecture of these ancient species along with those of their counterparts in the woodland garden—moss and mushrooms—create a fairy-tale landscape. The mysterious method of their propagation tells the story of evolution of life on the planet. Around since prehistoric times, ferns, mushrooms, and moss cast their spell over the Victorians and continue to entrance us to this day.

FERN STAND

MATERIALS

Wood column, minimum
  3' high, preferably with a
  square base
One 12"×12"×1½" bluestone
  paver
One 12"×12"×¾" bluestone
  paver
Three 5" lag bolts
All-purpose permanent
  adhesive, such as
  Quick-Grip

TOOLS

Pencil
Tape measure
Socket set
Miter saw
Drill
⅜" wood bit
Drill press
¾" and ⅜" masonry bits

 Victorian wood columns and pedestals are always a must-buy at tag sales and consignment shops because they elevate plants to new heights. Transforming a vintage column into a fern stand is a great way to highlight your favorite specimen ferns.

Making a beautiful object out of architectural salvage is not only green, it comes with its own patina. However, take care in picking out a salvaged column, avoiding any with lead paint.

A new column from a woodworking supply catalog can be used to similar effect. • *Photograph on page xviii*

1. Using miter saw, cut the column to desired height.

2. Set the thicker (1½") bluestone paver, which will be the base, on work surface with good side down and center column on base. Using pencil, trace outline of base onto stone; remove column. Mark 3 points inside the traced area of the column footprint. The 3 points should be in a triangular pattern, with each point at least 1" in from perimeter of tracing.

3. Connect ¾" masonry bit to drill press and position stone so that one of the marked points is directly under the bit. Drill down into the stone to a countersink depth of ½". This will allow heads of the lag bolts to sit flush with underside of stone base and will accommodate socket wrench head, so that lag bolt can be tightened to sit flush. Drill the other 2 marks in the same manner.

4. Connect ⅜" masonry bit to drill press. Drill through center of each of the holes created by the larger bit, until you have drilled through the stone. (You may do steps 3 and 4 in reverse if you find it easier. Whichever way you work, make sure smaller hole is at center of countersunk hole.)

5. Set the column upside down and center drilled stone on column base. Mark the center of each of the 3 holes on column with a pencil. Remove stone and drill a pilot hole at each of the three marks using ⅜" wood bit.

6. Apply permanent adhesive to bottom of wooden column base, following manufacturer's directions. Set stone base on column with the countersunk side of stone facing away from base. Next, use lag bolts and socket wrench to attach stone base to column. Allow to dry. Carefully invert the column and base right side up. Apply adhesive to top of column and set ¾" paver on top of column. Allow to dry.

   CAUTION The fern stand should never be picked up or moved by the stone top. Even though the adhesive may be strong, it is best to lift and move the column itself.

Eating seasonally connects us to the world around us, and each season brings its own bounty. Fiddlehead ferns, which are available only for a short time in the spring, are actually the unfurling fronds of the ostrich fern. (Other ferns are not edible.) If fiddleheads are out of season or are unavailable, asparagus can be substituted.

Beau Vestal of New Rivers Restaurant in Providence uses Verjus for this recipe. Verjus is the unfermented first pressing of the Chardonnay grape and is available at specialty shops. A good-quality white wine vinegar could be used in its place, but the subtle acidity of Verjus makes it an ideal flavoring in the dressing for this salad. With a simple salad such as this, it is the quality of the ingredients that brings it together.

SERVES 4

15 to 20 fresh fiddlehead ferns, cleaned and trimmed (see step 1)
4 to 6 cups fresh baby greens, such as a mesclun mix, cleaned and dried
4 to 6 tablespoons good-quality extra-virgin olive oil
1 cup pearl onions, skins removed
Coarse salt and freshly ground pepper to taste
4 to 6 tablespoons Verjus or white wine vinegar

1. Select tightly curled fiddleheads, rub off any brown coating, trim ends, and rinse under cool water.

2. Divide baby greens among 4 plates. Set aside.

3. Heat 2 to 3 tablespoons olive oil in a small sauté pan over medium heat. Add onions, toss and coat with oil, and then, after about 1 minute, add fiddlehead ferns, tossing constantly for another minute. Add salt and pepper to taste.

4. Remove from heat. Top salad greens with onions and fiddleheads.

5. To make the vinaigrette dressing, add Verjus to pan, place pan back over heat, and deglaze pan by swirling Verjus around and scraping up any browned bits from the bottom of the pan with a wooden spoon. Add more olive oil and Verjus to taste.

6. Pour dressing evenly over the 4 plates. Serve warm or, if you like, allow fiddleheads and onions to cool and divide over greens with vinaigrette just before serving.

Green roofs are gaining in popularity in the United States. Chicago, in fact, is starting to require them for large commercial projects. These living roofs help the environment in several ways. First, they insulate buildings better than standard asphalt roofs, holding in heat during cool weather and preventing heat from radiating down from a hot tar roof in summer. They also mitigate storm water runoff. Finally, the usual mixture of rooftops, sidewalks, and pavement absorb and radiate heat; as anyone who lives or works in a densely built city knows, the "urban heat island" effect drives temperatures up on hot summer days by as much as eight degrees compared with the outlying greener districts. But a green roof can mitigate heat as well as storm water; as more and more are built in our cities' downtowns, they'll help alleviate this problem.

Most of us are unable to convert the roofs of our homes to this energy-saving, environmentally friendly technology, but it is possible to bring the idea into our own backyard. When we were building a duck house on *Cultivating Life*, we thought we would engineer a small green roof of our own. With the help of green-roof expert Robert Herman, we came up with a project that would work well on any small outbuilding, provided the roof is properly waterproofed (we managed this by using an old pond liner as a waterproof membrane), has adequate drainage, and is capable of withholding the weight of the soil mix. And, though the environmental advantages of green roofs make them more than just something pretty to look at, they also provide one more place to grow plants, such as a mix of drought-tolerant hen and chicks, sedums, or hay-scented ferns.

BUILDING A SHED ROOF

As every shed is different in its specifications, we can merely give you the generic rules and guidelines that we used to build our roof.

Green roofs can be flat, slanted, or even gabled, but they all share a few characteristics. They need to be capable of holding the weight of the soil, plants, and water that will cover them. They need to be engineered to create adequate drainage so water that is not held in by expanded slate (a lightweight rock that helps keep growing mediums free-draining) can run off and not pool. They need to protect the building from water through the use of some waterproof material. Finally, they must be designed to avoid exposing surfaces that may rot to water.

For our duck house, a 2×4 frame was added around the edge of the roof and drilled drainage holes inserted on the lower edge (at the bottom of the slope).

Copper tubing was inserted in the holes to protect the surface of the wood. For waterproofing, the box and roof were fitted with an old pond liner. In turn, the pond liner was covered with a geotextile (permeable fabric that allows water and nutrients to pass through to soil, often referred to as landscape fabric), leaving an additional 14 inches of the geotextile along the bottom edge of the roof to create a drainage pocket and protect it from being damaged by roots or by the expanded slate. The inside of the pocket was filled with an 8-inch swath of ¼-inch gravel along the base of the roof. The geotextile was folded over the top of it and stapled into place to help prevent the drainage holes from being clogged by soil or roots as the green roof grows.

PLANTING A GREEN ROOF

1. To create growing medium, mix 4 parts of expanded slate or shale, which is lightweight and can absorb nutrients and water, with 1 part sterile organic soil. Expanded shale or slate can be bought online from green-roof companies.

2. Create a drainage strip (as for the roof) to protect the drainage holes from roots of plants.

3. Cover the remaining roof with a 3-inch layer of growing medium.

4. Set plants into the growing medium, making sure to place the crowns even with the top of the growing medium. Drought-tolerant plants such as *Sempervivum* (e.g., hen and chicks), the many members of the *Sedum* genus, and creeping thymes make excellent plants for this situation because they can handle the cycle of drought and rain that the roof receives naturally throughout the season, and will fill in quickly. Hay-scented fern (*Dennstaedtia punctiloba*) will also run across the roofline and is quite drought tolerant too. Full-size plants can be used, although commercial green-roof growers often use inexpensive plugs or small seedlings and water the roof for the first season in order to get the plants established.

The inherent beauty of the clean, straightforward lines of scientific equipment seems to cause us to observe things more closely. This simple vase made from test tubes and a petri dish is a wonderful way to highlight a variety of fern fronds or a collection of delicate blossoms from the garden. It's also a handsome object on its own.

1. Cluster test tubes in petri dish with tops up. You are trying to fit in as many as possible without overcrowding.

2. Stand group of test tubes upside down on table. Bundle together and place 2 rubber bands around bundle several inches apart to hold group together.

3. Invert bundle so that tops of test tubes are once again right side up. Make sure all the bottoms rest flat on the table.

4. Starting at an outer edge of petri dish, apply a thin line of epoxy in a spiral, turning dish until you have an even, shallow pool of glass glue in bottom of dish.

5. Set test tube bundle in dish. Check that all the tubes are flat in the dish and pressed into glue. Allow glue to set, following manufacturer's directions.

6. Fill the test tubes with water; then add young ferns or flowers.

MATERIALS
8 to 12 rimless test tubes
  (see step 1)
1 petri dish
2 rubber bands
Glass glue (epoxy)

NOTE
Always use epoxy in a well-ventilated area.

Anyone who has grown anything from seed can attest to the fact that the art of propagation is almost magical. Within that world, nothing is more mysterious than the methods involved in getting ferns to grow from spores. As nurseryman Tony Avent says, "When it comes to sex, ferns have it all backward." Ferns are nonflowering plants that reproduce through spores that form on the back of the individual fronds. But unlike other plants, ferns need to grow into mosslike prothalli before they can be fertilized (or, as Tony says, "have sex") and grow as ferns, which is why these plants were coveted by the Victorians—for their sexual timidity. But even in our more exhibition-istic times, ferns have an allure that makes them worth growing—and what modern-day gardener doesn't like a challenge?

1. In order to propagate ferns, collect mature spores off back of fern frond (they look like brown spots on the back of the frond and are typically ready to be harvested by midsummer). Put frond, along with spore cases, into an envelope and allow to dry for several days; the seed, which is nearly invisible to the human eye, will fall into the envelope. (If you look at the residue in the envelope with a magnifying glass, the spores are dustlike specks that are almost identical in size and form.)

2. Fill small plastic pot with soilless seed-starting mix. Pour boiling water into pot to sterilize soil and allow to cool. Sprinkle spores from envelope on top of potting medium in pot, tapping the envelope to remove all the spores. Put pot in a resealable plastic bag with a small hole pinched out in one corner of the bag for excess water runoff, and place in a warm spot with bright but not direct sunlight (a north- or east-facing window works well).

3. Set aside until a mosslike green substance forms on top of pot, taking care to make sure the potting medium does not dry out. This may take several months. If more water needs to be added to prevent drying out, use distilled water or boiled and cooled-down water to keep atmosphere sterile.

4. Once the mosslike substance has appeared, open bag and add a small amount of water to pot; swirl so that water circles around on top of mosslike substance. This will fertilize the developing prothalli.

5. Set aside (still in resealable plastic bag) until young sporelings start to sprout. When sporelings are 1 inch tall, separate and plant them in larger pots as you would small seedlings, being careful not to handle and damage young roots. Chopsticks can be used to separate sporelings by their fronds so as not to damage roots and a simple potting mix can be used to pot up plants into individual 2-inch pots. Keeping them in a humid environment such as a covered clear plastic shoebox as they grow will help ensure that they don't dry out.

6. As they increase in size, harden them up by increasing their exposure to a normal environment. Grow ferns in containers until plants are large enough to be set out in the garden.

FERN UNDER GLASS
Celebrating the form of a
favorite plant can be as simple
as pressing it between two
glass platters or plates and
using it as a seasonal serving
dish or charger.

MOSSY POTS

A patina of moss and lichen covering the outside of a terra-cotta container adds a special beauty and a sense of timelessness to any planting. Moss requires an acidic environment, which can be developed by brushing the exterior of a pot with buttermilk or yogurt and moss spores. Combine a small piece of moss from your garden with a cup or two of yogurt or buttermilk in a blender or food processor. Apply the mixture to the outside of the pot with a paintbrush, then put pot in a plastic bag to create a humid environment for moss to develop. Set in a cool, shady spot until moss begins to form. Plant container with moisture-loving plants and watch the moss thrive.

The fern case, as it was originally known, was invented by Dr. Nathaniel Ward, a British physician with a passion for botany and for ferns in particular. Despite his best efforts, Dr. Ward's ferns kept dying from what he believed to be the toxic air of nineteenth-century London during the Industrial Revolution. Ward was a plant enthusiast as well as an amateur lepidopterist working with butterflies, moths, and caterpillars. While experimenting with a cocoon in a covered jar, he noticed that several plants had grown in the bit of soil at the bottom of the jar, including a fern that seemed healthier than the ferns he was growing elsewhere. Ward began to build miniature greenhouses, in effect inventing the modern-day terrarium.

These Wardian cases were an important aid to early globe-trotting naturalists, enabling horticulturists to bring sensitive tropical plants back to Great Britain while protecting the plants from the salt air and the changing climate of seagoing vessels.

Wardian cases also became popular for growing plants. Although elaborate forms were built, simple jars and cloches over pots worked just as well. These days, it's not necessary to protect plants from toxic air, but overheated homes and central air-conditioning do dry them out. The sealed-in environment of Wardian cases provides the humidity certain plants need, allowing them to thrive on benign neglect. And, since moisture is trapped in the enclosed ecosystem, watering is rarely needed.

Wardian cases are ideal for plants such as ferns, miniature orchids, and begonias, which thrive in humid conditions and are well suited to nurturing miniature or dwarf plants, as they will not overgrow the cases. As long as soil and drainage are provided, plants should thrive. However, it is essential to place these containers in spots that are brightly lit but not in direct sunlight as the sun would heat up the container and bake the plants inside.

Victorians loved creating miniature universes within these cases. In that spirit, feel free to add stones, miniature bridges, or small containers to these *tableaux vivants*.

[CONTINUED]

MATERIALS

Wardian case, an aquarium with a glass top, a large jar with a lid, or a cloche with a pot underneath

Crushed gravel (enough for 3/4 inch bottom drainage layer in base of case)

Soilless potting medium

Charcoal chips, available at garden centers

Miniature plants such as begonias, ferns, peperomia, baby's tears, orchids, and Scotch mosses

Stones, decorative pieces, small containers (optional)

1. Whether you are planting a standard case with a planting tray or an old aquarium, creating adequate drainage is essential. On bottom of planting tray, aquarium, or jar, add a ¾-inch layer of gravel.

2. Add a thin layer of charcoal chips, enough to cover gravel. Top this off with 2 inches of potting mix. If potting a container to go into a case or under a cloche, add some charcoal to potting mix to keep the soil sweet and fresh. Create a hilly terrain by sloping potting mix up slightly toward center or back to help highlight the plantings. Keep Japanese gardens in mind as your aesthetic inspiration.

3. Begin setting in and arranging plants and any decorative details. If planting orchids, make sure they are terrestrial orchids; if not, set them in pots to allow for the proper growing medium. A mounted orchid can even be hung from side of case or set upright as an architectural element within case. Plant out arranged plants, making sure not to bury their crowns. Water lightly and put lid back on case.

4. The top of the case may have condensation from time to time, but that is merely the miniature ecosystem at work. If plantings seem waterlogged, open case and allow some of the humidity to evaporate and escape.

Growing under glass is a time-honored tradition and a wonderful way to get a closer look at the plant kingdom. Mosses have a special verdant beauty, with distinct structures that draw one in. Many of the less hardy species do well with this treatment. Since the spike mosses (*Selaginella*) pictured here will grow well enclosed in jars or Wardian cases, they make a perfect houseplant for those inclined to forget to water their plants. When grown in a glass jar or closed terrarium, they're basically maintenance free. They prefer indirect light and slightly damp (but not soggy) soil, and should be divided when they fill in too densely.

With more than 500 species native throughout the world (spike mosses hail from every continent except Antarctica), there's a great deal of diversity in selaginellas, from mossy green, chartreuse variegated forms to shimmering blue peacock moss. When it's time to divide, simply take out the plant, cut it into pieces, and replant. It is easy to start a new jar to pass along to a friend.

MATERIALS
Shadow box
Dried moss
Dried leaves, twigs,
    pods, pinecones,
    rocks, butterflies, etc.
Craft glue
Floral wire

TOOLS
Scissors
Wire cutters

 From the delicately articulated world of artist Joseph Cornell to collections of stones, twigs, and found objects from a child's pocket, shadow boxes create miniature universes that capture the imagination. This moss-lined box is the perfect way to bring a bit of nature into the home. The forms and colors of seedpods, twigs, dried flowers, and even an insect carcass can inspire us to look more closely at the world around us throughout the seasons. It's also fun to line the box with copies of topographical maps, geologic surveys, botanical drawings, stones, and dried herbarium specimens.

1. Remove the back of the shadow box frame.

2. Tear a piece of moss to roughly the size of the frame's back. Glue moss to frame's back.

3. Tear a piece or pieces of moss to fit inner sides of shadow box. Glue moss to inner sides.

4. When the inside of the frame is lined with moss, arrange your twigs, pods, pinecones, and other natural elements. Once arrangement is to your liking, attach elements to moss with craft glue and floral wire.

5. Replace the back of the frame.

6. To prevent bleaching, do not display the moss box in direct sunlight.

Botanical prints were originally developed in the seventeenth century to help scientists chronicle plant life, and they have been coveted by art collectors ever since for their beauty. Nowadays, with the use of color copiers and images available from the Internet, facsimiles of these valuable prints are a great resource for craft projects as well. You can enjoy the allure of these botanical prints on everyday items from coasters to platters. The finished plates also look great clustered on a table or hung on a wall.

The technique for these simple glass plates and platters is as simple as ordinary découpage, except that the image is set on the back of the glass plate, adhered with découpage medium, and then, for a more professional backing, either painted or covered in felt to protect the image further.

1. Clean back of plate to remove fingerprints and smudges. Using scissors, cut color copy of botanical print to a size slightly larger than the plate.

2. With a roller or paintbrush, apply a coat of découpage medium to the face of the image. Gently place image right side down against the back of the plate.

3. Carefully turn plate right side up and adjust image to desired position. Turn plate upside down again on work surface. Starting at center of back of plate, use the cork to rub and press the paper onto the back of the plate with circular motions to remove air bubbles.

4. When paper is completely adhered to plate, trim edges carefully with razor blade. Clear-coat back of plate with another layer of découpage medium. Set aside to dry.

5. Once dry, paint back with white latex primer to block finish color from showing through. (Spray paint or brushed-on paint works equally well for this.) Then paint back of plate with colored paint, if desired. Allow to dry.

6. A paint pen can be used to give the rim a finished look and to seal the paper's edge. (Metallic paint works well for this and adds a professional touch.) If desired, add adhesive felt to back of plate or seal with polyurethane for additional protection.

MATERIALS

Color copies of botanical prints
Smooth clear glass plates, platters, or coasters
Découpage medium
White latex primer and colored paint, spray or regular (optional)
Paint pen (optional)
Adhesive felt (optional)
Polyurethane sealer (optional)

TOOLS

Scissors
Small paint roller and paintbrushes
Razor blade
Cork

VEGETABLES

Defined simply as the edible part of a plant, vegetables are often viewed merely as economic crops, but their unmistakable beauty should not be overlooked. From the huge tropical-looking leaves of rhubarb and the vibrant hues of young lettuce to the towering forms of okra and pole beans, fresh-grown vegetables provide us not only with their unique flavors but also with a feast for the eyes.

MATERIALS

One 2"×6"×8' pine board
Five 1"×2"×8' pine boards
1½" galvanized finish nails
Exterior wood glue
Wood filler
Wood finish

TOOLS

Pencil
Tape measure
Carpenter's square
Hammer
1½" finish nails
Nail set
½" chisel
Drill
1/64" drill bit
Table saw
Miter saw
Palm sander
120 grit sandpaper
Two 24" Quick-Grip clamps

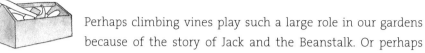

Perhaps climbing vines play such a large role in our gardens because of the story of Jack and the Beanstalk. Or perhaps there is something magical about the way pole beans pull themselves up toward the sky. Whatever the reason for our love of climbing vines, creating structures on which they can begin their ascent always takes hold of the gardener's imagination. These bean towers add structure and height to a garden and are ideal for planting anything from pole beans to flowering vines. Think about making more than one, because they look great in pairs and groups.

The design is simple and requires only a few tools. If you don't have a table saw, have the lumberyard rip the stock down for you. The best way of understanding how these come together is as a collection of mitered square frames attached to four supports on the inside edges of each frame's corner. The structure is then further strengthened with the addition of cross braces. • *Photograph on page 20*

1. Using the table saw, rip down the 2"×6"×8' pine board into four 1⅛"×1⅛"×8' (nominal) lengths. These will be used as the 4 poles.

2. Rip down the five 1"×2"×8' pine boards to ¾"×¾"×8' (nominal) lengths.

3. Set the miter saw to 45 degrees and cut 36 rails to ¾"×¾"×18" with the angles inward.

4. An additional 6 sections will need to be cut for the internal bracing; for accurate measurements, this can be done when they are ready to be installed. Sand all pieces and, if desired, apply a coat of stain or wood finish.

5. Place the 4 poles on a flat surface and clamp together. Measure 3 inches down from the top. This will be the mark for the top rail. Measure down and mark every 8¾ inches for each consecutive rail location. There will be a total of 9 rails; mark accordingly.

6. Separate 2 poles to the length of the short side of the angled rails. Place rails at marked location. Attach each rail to each pole with two 1½" finish nails. Repeat this process with the other 2 poles and 9 rails. Pilot holes should be drilled for each nail to prevent the wood from splitting. A dab of wood glue should be applied at all nailing locations to increase strength of the structure. Use nail set to ensure nails do not stick out.

7. Set the 2 completed sections on edge and attach the remaining rails, lining them up with the rails of each completed section.

8. The cross bracing can now be attached to the inside of the tower. This will require additional angled cuts. Each cross brace should be located at the top, middle, and bottom rail sections. Where the bracing crosses over itself, use a chisel to notch out the location of each overlap so that the two pieces recess into each other for a flush fit.

9. Use wood filler to fill each nail hole and allow to dry, lightly sand, and apply a second coat of stain to entire tower, if desired.

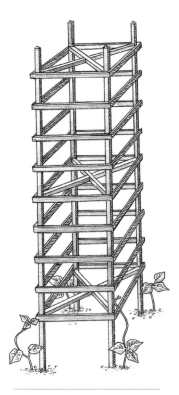

The crossbraces prevent racking

SERVES 6

FOR SEASONING PASTE

2-inch piece fresh ginger, peeled and chopped

3 garlic cloves

1 jalapeño pepper, seeded and chopped

1 teaspoon turmeric

1 teaspoon ground cumin

1/2 teaspoon ground fenugreek

1/2 teaspoon garam masala

1/4 cup freshly squeezed lime juice

FOR STIR-FRY

2 tablespoons peanut or vegetable oil

2 teaspoons black mustard seeds

1 white onion, thinly sliced

1 head cauliflower, cut into florets

1/2 pound fresh green beans, cut into 2-inch pieces

1/2 pound fresh wax beans, cut into 2-inch pieces

2 red or yellow peppers, cut into 1-inch squares

1/2 pound sugar snap peas, trimmed

1 cup diced plum tomatoes

Coarse salt

Beans, both shelled and fresh, are an important component of the global table. When cookbook author Aliza Green shared her Indian-inspired curry with us, she used the freshest beans available. The reason? The sugars in beans, like that of old-fashioned varieties of corn, quickly convert to starch after the beans are harvested.

1. Put all the ingredients for the seasoning paste in a food processor or blender. Puree until smooth. Set aside.

2. Heat the oil in a large skillet over medium heat. Add the mustard seeds, quickly cover pan, and cook until seeds begin to pop. Add onion and cook until softened, about 3 minutes. Add cauliflower, green beans, and wax beans, and cook 3 minutes more. Stir in the peppers and sugar snap peas.

3. Stir in the seasoning paste and cook for 5 minutes until vegetables are softened. Stir in tomatoes, season with salt to taste, and serve immediately.

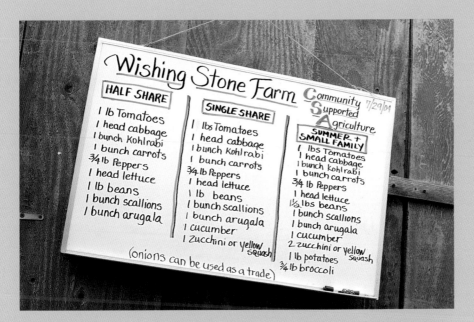

Though eating organic produce has been popular for some time, there is a growing movement to eat seasonally and locally, saving much of the biofuels used to ship produce across the country or import it from other parts of the world. This is especially so during the peak growing season, when local food should be readily available.

Even for people who are not growing their own vegetables, there is a way to eat locally and organically: CSAs, or Community Supported Agriculture programs. By committing upfront to a share in the farm's produce (shares come in a variety of sizes, suitable for one person or a whole family), people receive a weekly allotment of fresh vegetables and help support small local farms, many of which follow organic methods of farming. Some farmers even allow members to volunteer to work on the farm in order to lessen the cost of their share.

Picking up their weekly share from the CSA gives many customers a sense of community, as well as access to a wide array of vegetables not otherwise available to them. By cutting out the middleman, customers can often save money at the same time that they are supporting their local community. For local farmers Liz Peckham and Skip Paul at Wishing Stone Farm in Little Compton, Rhode Island, creating a CSA made running a small local farm economically viable.

An additional benefit of CSAs is that, because produce is grown locally, it can often be picked at its peak ripeness, as it does not need to survive the hardship of shipping. Many CSAs in more developed areas even deliver weekly to their customers, putting fresh produce as close as the kitchen door.

For more information on Community Supported Agriculture and to find a local CSA, visit localharvest.org.

MATERIALS

Two 2"×4"×10' cedar boards
Galvanized cattle fencing
    (6"×8" openings made
    of ³⁄₈"-diameter wire),
    sufficient for four 12"×72"
    panels
#10 stainless steel screws,
    2¹⁄₂" long
Exterior wood glue
Wood finish (optional)

TOOLS

Pencil
Miter saw with finish blade
Table saw with ripping blade
¹⁄₄" dado blade
Drill
Countersink drill bit
Framing square
Tape measure
36" Quick-Grip clamp
Palm sander
Bolt cutters

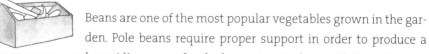

Beans are one of the most popular vegetables grown in the garden. Pole beans require proper support in order to produce a bumper crop, and providing rungs for the beans to attach to with their clinging tendrils will allow them to grow to amazing heights.

This architectural trellis would also be great for growing a decorative bean, such as the hyacinth bean, or even a vigorous clematis. The design is a simple rectangular box set on its end, with sides of cattle fencing. The large holes of the cattle fencing make it easy to harvest beans that grow on the inner vines. Making the frame of rot-resistant cedar will give the trellis a long life. It is a good idea to install the trellis when the beans are first planted so as not to damage the roots of the young plants.

1. Using the miter saw, cut both 2×4s into two 90" lengths and two 30" lengths. With the table saw, rip down all 4 lengths into 1½"×1½" posts. The longer pieces will be vertical posts and the shorter pieces will become crosspieces.

2. Set up a jig on your miter saw to hold a post perpendicular to the saw fence. Set miter angle to 10 degrees and cut bottom end of each 90" post 4 times to create a tapered point. This step is optional but will make it easier to install the tower.

3. Make a stop mark 74¾" down from top of each long post (i.e., mark will be closest to pointed end).

4. Create a groove on 2 adjacent sides of each long post; galvanized fencing will rest in these slots. Install ¼" dado blade in table saw and set the fence ⅜" from blade. With blade set to a depth of ½", cut a groove lengthwise down post from top to stop mark. Set fence ¹⁵⁄₁₆" from the blade, turn the post a quarter turn, and cut a groove down the length of the adjacent side.

5. Using bolt cutters, cut 4 panels of galvanized wire, each 2 squares by 9 squares. Leave ½" of wire ends around the perimeter of the 4 sides of each panel.

6. Insert first panel section into the groove of a post; slide another post onto the opposite side of panel. Align posts and clamp in place.

7. Using miter saw, cut one of the 2'6" lengths into two 12⁵⁄₁₆" crosspieces. Set the rip fence on your table saw ¼" from dado blade and groove each crosspiece to receive the wire ends.

8. Glue the ends of a crosspiece and slide it—groove side up—over bottom edge of wire panel. Bottom edge of crosspiece should be 75¾" from the top. Drill pilot hole through post into each side of crosspiece, countersink holes, and secure with 2½" stainless steel screws. Install top crosspiece, aligning flush with top of posts.

9. Repeat steps 6 through 8 to construct second panel.

10. Assemble the structure by attaching two remaining wire panels to two finished sides completed in steps 1–9.

11. Cut remaining two 30" lengths into 4 crosspieces and dado grooves, as in step 7. Install remaining crosspieces with glue and screws, as in step 8.

12. Allow glue to dry, lightly sand trellis, and apply finish of choice. Or leave unfinished to weather to a silvery gray.

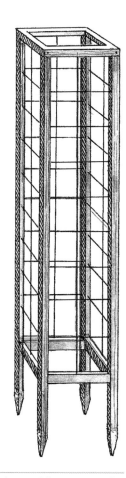

Galvanized fencing gives this trellis added strength

BEAN VOTIVES

Although heirloom beans are a beautiful addition to any garden, it's probably been a few decades since anyone considered decorating with them. Nevertheless, when offset by a tea light and a simple flameproof glass, these colorful legumes add a nice finishing touch to a table setting.

portable salad table

Gardeners are always looking for new ways to fit more plants into their lives, and University of Maryland agricultural extension agent Jon Traunfeld is no exception. Not only does his portable salad table allow people to grow greens wherever they live, it is also easy to build and transport. That means it can be moved into a protected area when necessary to extend the growing season as long as possible. By growing cut-and-come-again crops of spinach, lettuce, and other leafy greens, and the occasional reseeding of this small table garden, you can make sure you and your loved ones get their daily greens for months on end. The tray can be set up on sawhorses, so that caring for and harvesting it can be done without constant bending—which is especially nice at the end of a long day of work in the perennial garden.

Jon has also built customized forms of this table for growing tomatoes and cucumbers in sizes that are suited to any space. This version is 58 inches long by 33 inches wide, with a 3½-inch depth perfectly suited to growing lettuce.

The table is a simple frame with a mesh base to hold soil but allow water to drain off, allowing lettuce to thrive in the conditions it loves. Because the crops harvested will be eaten, use untreated framing lumber.

1. Using a miter saw, cut two 58" lengths out of one 10' 2×4 to make the long sides of the tray. Cut four 30" lengths from the other 10' 2×4 to serve as crosspieces.

2. Using 3" galvanized screws, attach the 58" long sides to the 30" crosspieces, predrilling holes to avoid splitting wood. The 2 interior crosspieces are attached 18¾" from each end of the long piece, to create 3 equal planting sections.

3. Center window screening on outside bottom of frame. Stretch it tautly over frame (a second set of hands is helpful for this), fold excess screening evenly up sides of frame, and staple it to the frame bottom and sides using a staple gun.

4. Center hardware cloth over the window screening, pull taut, and staple to bottom of frame. Use roofing nails and hammer to nail hardware cloth to bottom of frame for additional support. Use tin snips to cut out each corner of hardware cloth and fold over sides of frame. Secure to sides with staples and roofing nails. Set on sawhorses and prepare for planting (see below).

MATERIALS

2 untreated 2"×4"x10'

#2 galvanized Phillips screws, 3" long

3'×5' piece of aluminum window screening

⅜" staples

3'×5' piece of ½" mesh hardware cloth

Roofing nails

Sawhorses on which to set finished table

TOOLS

Miter saw

Hammer

Staple gun

Screwdriver

Drill

Tin snips

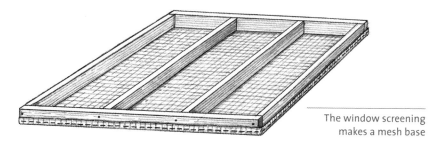

The window screening makes a mesh base

PLANTING A SALAD TABLE

1. Select a level location to set out salad table. Make sure there is easy access to water so plants can be irrigated regularly. Salad greens grow best in full sun in cooler weather. As weather becomes hot, move to a shadier spot, since too much sunlight will make greens bolt or go to seed.

2. Fill frame with potting mix and create shallow furrows in each compartment about 4 to 5 inches apart. Sow seeds about 1 inch apart and water in well. If plants are too close together, any thinnings can be harvested young and used as baby greens. Most seeds will germinate in 2 to 3 days. Keep soil evenly moist.

3. Harvest as needed. By cutting some greens with scissors, you should be able to get several harvests from one planting before needing to sow fresh seed.

MATERIALS

Seeds of a variety of greens, including lettuce, spinach, mustard, cabbage, radishes, beet greens, mizuna, mâche, and cress

Organic time-release fertilizer or cottonseed meal

Potting mix

Cold frames have so many uses: starting and hardening off seedlings, planting with cool-weather greens for harvesting off season, and protecting tender perennials and annuals before they can be set outdoors (for additional uses, see page 34). By opening and closing the top to varying degrees, the temperature inside the frame can be regulated, giving a gardener a rare upper hand against Mother Nature.

This version cuts the cost of materials by repurposing a tempered storm door—look for one at a junkyard. The money you save allows you to splurge on cedar for the sides of the frame, guaranteeing that it will be around for years to come.

1. Remove tempered glass from the door frame. The size of the glass will determine the width and length of the cold frame. Our glass measured 30³/₄"×74³/₄" and all measurements for this project are based on this glass size, but they can be adjusted to meet the size of any glass panel.

2. Build frame around glass. (Our glass had a gasket around the entire edge that was kept in place to provide a snug fit into the new cedar frame.) Using miter saw, cut two 2×4s to 79" and one 2×4 to two 35" pieces. The remaining 2×4 will be used later.

   Using table saw, rip down all the 79" and 35" pieces to a width of 2¹/₂". Using miter saw, cut down these pieces to a finished dimension of 78" and 34" respectively. Using miter saw, make 45-degree cuts at ends to create mitered corners for frame.

3. On table saw, set up a ³/₈" dado blade with a height of ⁷/₈ inch. (This measurement will create a notch in frame to accept glass and gasket.) Set saw fence so center of dado blade is centered on 1¹/₂" side of the frame stock. Run interior 1¹/₂" side of each piece over dado to create a groove in the center of the frame. Slide 4 sides of frame into place for a snug fit. Once properly fit, fasten corners with exterior-grade wood glue and 1¹/₂" stainless steel screws. Predrill and countersink all screw holes for plugs later. Set aside and build box for cold frame.

4. Using miter saw, cut 5 lengths of 78" from 1×6 cedar boards and cut 1 length of 78" from the 1"×10"×12' cedar board. The remainder of stock will be used for the sides of the cold frame. Cut two 12¹/₂" pieces, one 11" piece, and three 25" pieces of 2×4 as braces for the front and back of frame. Trim 1 end of each of the 12¹/₂" and 25" pieces of 2×4 to an angle of 30 degrees. Using table saw, rip down the 78" length of 1×10 to a 30-degree angle on one edge of the length of the board. Remove just enough material to accomplish this. This board will be placed on the top back side of cold frame and the beveled edge will allow the door to sit flush when closed. This is the angle at which the glass door will slope.

[CONTINUED]

MATERIALS

Glass storm door with
    tempered glass
Four 2"×4"×8' cedar boards
Three 1"×6"×12' cedar boards
Two 1"×6"×8' cedar boards
One 1"×10"×12' cedar board
1¹/₂" stainless steel screws
Three 3" exterior grade T-hinges
Two 6" exterior-grade handles
Exterior wood glue
2 "touch-and-hold" door
    closers (such as those used
    on a screen door to prevent
    slamming)
Two 14" stakes

TOOLS

Table saw
Miter saw
³/₈" dado blade
Drill
Countersink drill bit
Plug cutter
Coping saw
Screw gun
Tape measure
Framing square
Palm sander
Fine-grade sandpaper

NOTES

Pilot holes should be drilled
    prior to screwing to prevent
    the wood from splitting.
All screws that will be
    noticeable on the
    finished product must be
    countersunk for insertion
    of plugs later on.
The addition of wood glue to all
    joints will strengthen them.

favorite uses for cold frames

- Starting seeds and protecting young seedlings from frost cycle
- Growing cool-season vegetables as late into the season as possible
- Moving along forced bulbs in the early spring while still being able to regulate the temperature in order to prevent them from coming on too fast
- Giving dry heat to dormant South African bulbs during the summer months
- Setting over a vegetable bed to warm soil and get plants such as tomatoes into the ground a little ahead of the game
- Protecting onions and garlic from rain while curing
- Drying chilies and making sun-dried tomatoes for long storage

5. Lay out three 11½" pieces of 2×4 with the angled edge sloping down and away. Set two 78" boards across 2×4s and set in outer 2×4s ¾" from edge of 78" boards to accommodate side panels of frame for a flush finish. The third 2×4 should be centered. Attach two 78" boards to 2×4s from the bottom up. The screws are countersunk from the exterior.

6. Lay out three 2"×4"×25" pieces with angled edges sloping up and away. Each end 2×4 should be set in ¾" to accept the side panels for a flush finish. The third 2×4 should be centered. Attach three of the 78" boards to the 2×4s from the bottom up. Attach the 1×10 last, making sure the beveled edge runs in the same direction as the angled end of the 2×4s.

7. Given our slope angle of 30 degrees and the finished width of glass door at 34", the sides of our cold frame will be 31". From remaining 1×6 stock, cut 6 lengths of 29½ inches (the width minus thickness of front and back panels). Attach 2 bottom side boards at each end to connect front and back panels.

8. Position third board of side panel in place and mark a 30-degree angle from front of frame, sloping back. Trace this measurement to 1×6 side panel for other side, cut both to size, and attach to each end respectively. Repeat this process for final 1×10 side boards, continuing upward 30-degree slope. The top side board should sit flush with top of back panel. Fasten these last 2 panels to back panel 2×4s and also screw front of these last two side panels down from top into the side panel board below. Be sure to set screw back a good inch from narrow point to prevent splitting of wood.

9. Lay door on top of frame and attach T-hinges to both frame and door. Position T-hinges so that screws will fasten to 2×4s. Add 2 handles to front of the door in a convenient location for opening and closing.

10. Attach door closers. For our project, touch-and-hold door closers were used to prop open the door while adding and removing plants. Be sure the door closers used are rated for the weight of the finished door. (An alternative, less expensive, option is to use a 1" dowel or similar size hardwood cut to size to prop open door.)

11. Use plug cutter to fill countersink screwholes, cut flush with coping saw, and sand smoothly.

12. Set in place. Once in place, 2 stakes should be driven into the ground just inside front panels. The stakes should be fastened to cold frame to prevent door from tipping entire frame backward when the door is opened.

For many of us, the thought of building anything—let alone an elaborate-looking potting bench or a cold frame—is beyond the scope of what we imagine to be our abilities. It certainly requires tools beyond those gathering dust in our basements, storage lockers, and garages. But in the same way that back in fifth grade shop class we were able to fashion a toolbox out of pine—something that had at first seemed beyond our ability—so many of these projects are surprisingly doable.

Some of the woodworking projects in this book require the use of a miter saw or table saw. However, if you don't have such equipment you can have wood precut to specifications at a hardware store or ripped down to size at a lumberyard, or you may even take advantage of the local high school shop or a craftier friend to mill things to size. And unless otherwise specified, a general-purpose blade on your miter or table saw will do the trick for these projects just fine.

The use of simple connection joints such as a rabbet joint—which can be cut with an old-fashioned shoulder plane, made with a router, or created with single or multiple passes on a table saw fit with a dado blade (the easiest of the three methods)—means we don't have to understand the intricacies of mortise-and-tenon joinery in order to make what appears to be a fine piece of furniture.

The projects in this book were developed with the television show *Cultivating Life* in mind and we have tried to limit the tools to ones that are fairly easy to get your hands on. There are no $200,000 laser planers used, just a palm sander and some straightforward techniques to make your work look its best. Whether it's simply countersinking screws and plugging the holes to cover them up or easy-to-cut butt joints to frame a stone-topped table, these processes require more patience than skill. Once you have mastered them, like the proverbial bike, you will remember how to do them again for years to come.

And like the first ride on your bike, your sense of accomplishment will have you grinning from ear to ear.

This cedar table was one of the first projects we shot in the initial season of *Cultivating Life*. The crew immediately recognized its versatility—it can be a workbench, a place to pot plants, the perfect area to prepare food, or an outdoor bar. As the shooting season progressed, various crew members cornered our craftsman, Eric Piotte, who built the table on-air, to talk them through the project. Everyone was convinced they had to have one.

Although the joinery looks complex and the trim has the appearance of having been crafted by a master woodworker, the project is straightforward to build. The table itself is made up of 3 components: the top, the shelf, and the legs. Precutting components makes assembly easy.

FOR THE TOP

Using miter saw, cut two 2"×4"×8' to $93\frac{1}{2}$" long.

Cut the 2"×4"×12' to two 30" lengths and three 27" lengths.

Using table saw, notch out the ends of the 30" sections to create a rabbet joint by removing $\frac{3}{4}$"×$1\frac{1}{2}$"×$3\frac{1}{2}$".

Rip down two of the 27" boards in half lengthwise to four $1\frac{1}{2}$"×2"×27" (nominal) sections.

Using either saw, cut two 4" lengths out of the 2"×4"×10'.

Rip down the two 4" lengths in half lengthwise into four $1\frac{1}{2}$"×2"×4" (nominal).

Cut seven of the 1"×6"×8' to $\frac{5}{8}$"×$5\frac{1}{2}$"×95" (nominal).

Rip down one $\frac{5}{8}$"×$5\frac{1}{2}$"×95" to three $\frac{5}{8}$"×1"×95" lengths.

Cut one $\frac{5}{8}$"×1"×95" into two $\frac{5}{8}$"×1"×33" lengths.

FOR THE SHELF

Using miter saw, cut the remaining two 2"×4"×8' to $90\frac{1}{4}$" long.

Cut the remaining 2"×4"×10' to two 23" lengths and three 20" lengths.

Notch the ends of the 23" sections with table saw to create a rabbet joint by removing $\frac{3}{4}$"×$1\frac{1}{2}$"×$3\frac{1}{2}$" of material.

Rip one 20" board in half lengthwise to two $1\frac{1}{2}$"×2"×20" (nominal).

Cut four 1"×6"×8' to $\frac{5}{8}$"x $5\frac{1}{2}$"×$90\frac{1}{2}$" (nominal).

Rip down two $\frac{5}{8}$"×$5\frac{1}{2}$"×$90\frac{1}{2}$" into:

Two $\frac{5}{8}$"×3"×$90\frac{1}{2}$" and two $\frac{5}{8}$"×2"×$90\frac{1}{2}$"

Rip down one $\frac{5}{8}$"×$5\frac{1}{2}$"×$90\frac{1}{2}$" into:

One $\frac{5}{8}$"×2"×$90\frac{1}{2}$" and two $\frac{5}{8}$"×1"×$84\frac{7}{8}$"

Rip down one $\frac{5}{8}$"×$5\frac{1}{2}$"×$90\frac{1}{2}$" into:

Two $\frac{5}{8}$"×2"×$90\frac{1}{2}$" and two $\frac{5}{8}$"×$\frac{5}{8}$"×23"

[CONTINUED]

MATERIALS

Four 2"×4"×8' cedar boards

One 2"×4"×12' cedar board

One 2"×4"×10' cedar board

Eleven 1"×6"×8' cedar boards

One 4"×4"×12' cedar post

$2\frac{1}{2}$", 3", $1\frac{5}{8}$", and $1\frac{1}{2}$" stainless steel screws

Exterior wood glue

Water-repellent sealer

Heavy-duty rubber mat (optional)

TOOLS

Tape measure

Carpenter's square

Flush-cut pull saw

Drill

$\frac{3}{32}$" drill bit

Screw gun

$\frac{3}{32}$" countersinking drill set

Table saw with finish blade

Miter saw with finish blade

Two 4' bar clamps

Drill press

$\frac{3}{8}$" plug cutter

Palm sander

150 grit sandpaper

NOTES

Pilot holes should be drilled prior to screwing to prevent the wood from splitting.

All screws that will be noticeable on the finished product should be countersunk for insertion of plugs later on.

The addition of wood glue to all joints will strengthen them.

Cut the 4"×4"×12' post into four 35³⁄₈" lengths.

Notch out the end of one side of each post, removing 3¹⁄₂"×3¹⁄₂"×1¹⁄₂" of material.

This notch will allow the top frame to rest on each leg for added support.

1. Begin by assembling the tabletop frame. Piece together the 93¹⁄₂" and 30" notched 2×4s into a rectangle using 2¹⁄₂" screws. Next, attach the 27" 2×4 on the inside frame, centered, with the 3¹⁄₂" side (nominal) faceup and flush with the top of the frame. Add the remaining 1¹⁄₂"×2"×27" sections in the same way, evenly spaced, making sure the 2" side is faceup.

2. Attach each of the 4 legs to the frame. The notch on each leg should face out to the long side of the frame and fit flush with the frame. Use four 3" screws at each side of the frame for attachment to the leg. Attach the remaining 1¹⁄₂"×2"×4" bracing against each leg on the inside frame on the long end and flush with the top.

A rabbet joint connects two boards at a right angle by removing the portion of one of the boards to accommodate the other board; it's easily made on a table saw fit with a dado blade. Screws can be countersunk and covered with plugs to create a more finished look.

3. Next, assemble the shelf. Piece together the 90¼" and 23" notched 2×4s into a rectangle using 2½" screws. Attach the two 20" 2×4s on the inside frame, spaced evenly apart, with the 3½" side faceup and flush with the top of the frame. Add the 2 remaining 1½"×2"×20" sections to the end of each side of the frame, making sure the 2" side is faceup and flush with the frame top.

4. Attach the shelf to the legs using 3" screws, screwing from the inside out to the leg. The base of the shelf frame should be 10" from the floor.

5. Using the 1½" and 1⅝" screws, attach from the underside the ⅝"×3"×90½" boards to the end of either side of the shelf frame. The ends of each of these boards are notched so that they fit flush with the table legs. Next, evenly space out the 5 remaining ⅝"×2"×90½" sections. There should be a 1½" gap between each section. Use the ⅝"×⅝"×23" sections as trim at each end. The two ⅝"×1"×84⅞" pieces should be secured to the 2×4 frame between the table legs, underneath the overhanging ⅝"×3"×90½" boards.

6. Assemble the five ⅝"×5½"×95" boards to the top of the table. Secure these boards together with bar clamps and center them on the frame. Using the 1½" and 1⅝" screws, attach the tabletop to the frame from the underside. Use the ⅝"×2"×33"sections as trim at each end. The two ⅝"×1"×95" pieces should be fastened to the 2×4 frame underneath the overhanging tabletop.

7. Using leftover material from the 1×6 pieces and a ⅜" diameter plug cutter, make plugs to fill in the countersunk screws. Apply wood glue and lightly tap into place. Use a flush-cut pull saw to cut off any excess and lightly sand the entire table. Apply wood finish of choice.

8. For exterior use of furniture, the addition of rubber matting to the foot of each leg is recommended.

MATERIALS

Seeds of a variety of greens,
    including lettuce, spinach,
    mustard, cabbage, radishes,
    beet greens, mizuna,
    mâche, and cress
Organic time-release fertilizer
    or cottonseed meal
Potting mix

For many people who are considering planting a vegetable garden, facing a bare plot of land each spring that's in need of cultivation and planting can be daunting. But for gardeners in the know, a few perennial crops that come back year after year (such as asparagus, horseradish, and rhubarb) help make the early-season garden seem a little less barren—and often provide interesting flowers or foliage for the vegetable garden all season long. The trick to growing perennial vegetables, like that of a perennial flower garden, lies in good soil preparation. Tilling the soil deeply and amending it with well-rotted manure and compost will guarantee robust crops for seasons to come.

Rhubarb is incredibly easy to grow. It can be harvested from mid-spring (and even earlier in the season if you're using a rhubarb forcer) to early summer. A rhubarb forcer is a terra-cotta cylinder that is set over the crown of the plant in early spring and helps gives the crop an early start while also helping to lengthen the delicious stalks. Once the stalks have developed leaves out of the top of the cylinder, the forcer can be removed and the stalks harvested.

It's also important to keep perennial vegetables well fertilized and to control the weeds around the plants. If you can keep up maintenance until at least August 15, the plants will grow well for the season. Whether you are planting asparagus, horseradish, rhubarb, or Jerusalem artichokes (which are perennial sunflowers with beautiful yellow blooms and an edible root), site them carefully in the garden—remember, they will remain in that location for years to come.

PLANTING ASPARAGUS

A mature bed of asparagus is a vegetable gardener's delight, but it takes patience to establish the bed, as the planting procedure is time-consuming. Organic gardener Skip Paul suggests harvesting a little the first year after planting because "you worked hard and deserve the reward," but allowing a good portion of the first year's crop to go to seed will help establish the bed for years to come. In addition, the tall ferny stalks of asparagus in seed add a wonderful romantic look to the vegetable garden. Asparagus rootstock is typically bought in the spring and set out in an already prepared bed.

1. Dig a trench about 4 inches deep.

2. Start at one end of the trench and spread out the roots of each piece of stock so they are fanned out in several directions. Space the plants 14 inches apart.

3. Take a mixture of manure and compost and crumble over the roots. Add about 1 inch of soil and water.

4. Allow the plant to grow for about 3 weeks. Then add another inch of manure mixture and soil.

5. Repeat every 3 weeks until the trench is covered.

6. Harvest only 25 percent of the crop the first year. This will allow the plant to establish. In subsequent years, remember that if you fertilize asparagus, it does not need a lot of nitrogen. Phosphorus and potassium are more important.

PLANTING HORSERADISH

Horseradish is incredibly vigorous and can easily overtake a garden. The best way to grow it is to create a divider in the soil that limits its spread. A large nursery container (the size for a large shrub or tree) with its bottom cut out is ideal for this.

1. Dig a hole big enough to bury the container.

2. Fill the bottom of the container with the excavated soil. Add compost in the bottom. Plants eat from the bottom up.

3. Remove the topsoil of the horseradish, which could contain weeds. Fill in around the plant with soil.

PLANTING RHUBARB AND JERUSALEM ARTICHOKES

Rhubarb and Jerusalem artichokes are simply planted out as tubers or rootstock in early spring, in a garden bed whose soil has been amended with compost and watered in. Harvesting for Jerusalem artichokes can begin that fall, and rhubarb should be established by the following spring. Like horseradish, Jerusalem artichokes may spread, so site wisely.

OUTDOOR KITCHEN

Perhaps the idea of cooking outdoors connects us to our primitive roots and centuries of hunting and gathering, but since it allows us to come together and make meals with friends and family on a beautiful day, the outdoor kitchen also connects us to another tradition: preparing and sitting down to meals in the company of those we love. And if we can spend the day out in the garden using fresh herbs right from the garden, why not?

The kitchen always has a way of drawing people in during a party or family gathering, and an outdoor kitchen is no exception. Whether it is a simple table and outdoor grill on a deck (could the smell of anything cooking on the grill be more alluring?) or a more complex arrangement of counters, a small refrigerator, and a sink with running water to complement the grill, it will become a destination spot in the backyard.

Many of the same decisions that take place in designing an indoor kitchen apply to outdoor kitchens as well. Some advance planning and careful evaluation of the right questions will help ensure that each cook ends up in an outdoor kitchen that's suited to his or her individual needs as closely as possible. • *Photograph on page 42*

BUDGET

Like any home improvement project, from building a terrace to redoing a bathroom, setting a budget helps determine the scope of the project. Outdoor kitchens can run the gamut from several thousand dollars to six figures for the most obsessed barbecuer. Although it is ideal to do all the work at once, outdoor kitchens are better suited to stages than most home improvement projects, provided the final product is planned out and the steps are taken in an order that minimizes the need to redo any of the work. Although buying a big grill may seem like the first step, in fact, setting up access to electricity, natural gas (where available and to code for outdoor grills), and potable water should be the first priority—even before a terrace is laid. (Remember, great meals can be cooked on a hibachi, but you aren't going to wash dishes with a hose and a tub of cold soapy water.) Amenities such as a pizza or tandoor oven can always be added later, provided room was left for them in the plan.

SITING

Though it seems that it might be common sense to have an outdoor kitchen just outside the kitchen door, consider other factors when locating an outdoor kitchen. Being near the house can save money by providing easier access to water, sewer lines, and electricity (and means not having to lug things back and forth to the house across the lawn), but consider whether the outdoor kitchen would be better near the vegetable garden, in a spot with a beautiful view, or near the area on the terrace or deck where guests will be congregating while dinner is being made. Just as the family room has been incorporated into the indoor kitchen, a sitting area or island near the grill can mean having a chance to catch up with guests while flipping a few steaks on the grill. And sitting down to dinner away from the house increases the chance of not hearing the phone ring when another telemarketer calls.

ADDITIONAL USES

An outdoor sink and workspace can have innumerable uses beyond putting together a meal, so think about how the space might also be employed. Should you plan for storage for potting equipment, a painting station, or a clothesline or drying spot for hand washables?

FLEXIBILITY

Many kitchens are locked in place by stationary counters and appliances. Whereas the sink and refrigerator may be best placed permanently, you might want to leave your grill mobile so that when a prevailing wind changes direction, the grill can be moved to keep the smoke from blowing in the wrong direction. Placing a worktable such as a cedar potting bench across from an island with a sink and the refrigerator (sided by a counter with stools) gives you the best of both worlds, allowing for maximum flexibility in reengineering the space for a cocktail party or casual dinner.

PROTECTION FROM THE ELEMENTS

There is great pleasure in eating and cooking outdoors, but no one wants to be overwhelmed by glaring sunlight or the wind, or to burn their hand on a scalding hot countertop. In warmer climates, be careful to site the kitchen where the sun can be minimized or consider putting it underneath a lath structure or roof, being sure to have adequate ventilation for smoke from the grill. An icemaker that gets hit by the afternoon sun is going to have to work awfully hard. In cooler climates, think about siting the kitchen so that it benefits from the radiant heat of a stone wall or the side of your house; this will help extend the grilling season. In windy areas, consider adding infrared burners rather than the traditional gas ones, which tend to blow out. And, when selecting countertop materials,

be sure to consider how well they will stand up to the local climate—and how much heat they will absorb.

In addition, special care should be used in choosing materials that are able to sustain the elements. For the outdoor kitchen we use on *Cultivating Life*, stainless steel appliances, yellow cypress cabinets, and a soapstone countertop and sink have shown themselves to hold up well to the elements.

FOOD AND EQUIPMENT STORAGE

As with any task, cooking outdoors is made easiest by having all equipment at your fingertips. Be sure to plan for storage for pots and pans, utensils and dishes, and possibly even a spice drawer to hold a few favorite spice rubs. Make sure they are designed to be weatherproof and, if young children are at hand, consider having a few drawers that lock to hold knives or other sharp objects.

PLUMBING AND ELECTRICAL

Consult with an electrician and a plumber regarding electrical and plumbing concerns as early as possible in the planning stage. Building codes vary from place to place, as do weather considerations for outdoor plumbing and sewer lines, and it is best to know the rules before plotting out a dream kitchen.

SPECIAL AMENITIES

Don't forget to consider a few amenities that may seem luxurious but are a personal priority. Pizza and tandoor ovens, icemakers, a dishwasher, or even a margarita machine may seem indulgent, but if they serve your needs, they warrant consideration.

BARBECUE TRUG

A simple wooden tool carrier is easily repurposed as a handy grill kit that gets everything out to the grill with the use of one hand. Several pairs of tongs, a bottle of olive oil, bamboo skewers, a small cutting board, and a knife are snuggled in with a favorite grill rub, salt and a pepper mill, a wooden juicer, and a few kitchen towels, keeping the other hand free for carrying a platter of steaks or vegetables for grilling.

This caddy was designed for silverware, but it can easily be reworked into a trug for transporting everything from favorite condiments and barbecue supplies to art supplies for kids or an aspiring artist.

MATERIALS

One $\frac{1}{2}$"×$5\frac{1}{2}$"×7' oak board

7 stainless steel screws, $1\frac{5}{8}$" long

Wood glue

Wood stain or finish

TOOLS

Pencil

Tape measure

Miter saw

Table saw

Jigsaw

Drill

Countersink drill bit

Bit for pilot holes

Sandpaper

2 Quick-Grip clamps

Screwdriver

Scrap wood (to press the trim pieces into place while glue dries)

1. Using table saw, cut the $\frac{1}{2}$"×$5\frac{1}{2}$" oak board into three 11" lengths (used for ends, handle, and trim to cover screws), four 9" lengths (used for sides, middle divider, and bottom), and two 2" lengths (used for remaining inside dividers).

2. Rip down one of the $5\frac{1}{2}$"×11" lengths into one 9"×$1\frac{1}{2}$"×$\frac{1}{2}$" board (used for handle), two 11"×$\frac{3}{16}$"×$\frac{1}{2}$" strips (used as trim), and four $6\frac{1}{2}$"×$\frac{3}{16}$"×$\frac{1}{2}$" strips (used as trim).

3. Sketch out and shape two $5\frac{1}{2}$"×11" boards to be used as ends. Measure up 6 inches from bottom of board and mark left and right sides at this height. Then find center point at top of board and place a mark $\frac{3}{4}$" on either side of center mark. Connect top left mark to left side mark and repeat on right side of board using an arcing line. Be sure both sides are symmetrical. The handle will be connected to these boards. Clamp a second 11" board to the one with the pattern and cut out shape using the jigsaw.

4. Begin assembly. With any hardwood such as oak, pilot holes should be drilled to prevent wood from splitting when screws are inserted. Pilot holes should be the diameter of the screw, minus the turned bits that will lock screw in place. Countersink holes. Attach two ends to bottom 9"×$5\frac{1}{2}$" board with glue and screws. The bottom should butt up against back side of each end. Screws should be inserted at either side of end and in center. Be cautious when positioning screws so that $\frac{1}{2}$"-wide strips will cover all the screw holes during final assembly. Countersink screw holes.

5. Fasten both 9"×$5\frac{1}{2}$" sides with glue and screws, being sure screw holes are aligned at either side of caddy ends. Attach the 9"×$5\frac{1}{2}$" center divider, being sure it is centered in caddy box.

6. Add remaining two 2" dividers to one side of caddy, also spacing them equally apart. These two smaller pieces will be fastened only with wood glue.

7. Attach handle $\frac{1}{2}$" down from top of each end, taking care to center it. The handle should be in alignment with center divider in caddy.

8. Cut to size and glue on trim pieces to cover all exposed screws. The trim should run the length of the caddy ends, with the side pieces flush with the corners and the middle trim centered. To hold strips in place, sandwich caddy between 2 pieces of scrap wood and clamp together.

9. Sand the caddy so that all edges are smoothed over. Apply finish of choice.

CHICKEN WIRE ARMOIRE

It's a tall order to come up with an outdoor cupboard that provides protection from animals as well as enough air circulation to prevent the buildup of mold and mildew from trapped moisture. However, by simply taking out the front panels of a ready-made cupboard from an unfinished furniture store and replacing them with coated chicken wire, you can create the perfect storage unit for dishes, kitchen towels, and even a few dry goods. Place it under an overhang within a few steps of the outdoor kitchen.

Anna Atkins (1799–1871) was a pioneer in the field of cyanotypes in the 1850s. She created a stunning collection of images of British algae with this process, which uses the sun to create photographic images.

The formula and chemicals used in this process have evolved over the years, so that the materials are now more environmentally friendly and easy to use. It is fun to document the plants from your garden in this manner and gives you another way to see natural forms. Paper-based sun prints are great for framing, while fabric-based ones make perfect tablecloths, pillows, and napkins. The possibilities are endless—you can even have your own clothing, fabric, and paper treated, rather than buying what is available commercially.

1. Work indoors, away from any direct sunlight or in a shady spot, and prepare plant cuttings for laying out on paper or sun print fabric. They may be fresh or pressed and dried.

2. Lay board down on a flat surface with piece of corrugated cardboard on top of board. Open sealed bag containing sun print material and arrange leaves or flowers on sun print material (indoor light will not cause exposure to begin; UV light is required to react with chemicals). Either pin plants to surface of treated material or cover with a pane of glass. Keep in mind that the angle of the sun may create strong shadows from pins, causing them to show up on final print when finished.

3. Expose material to UV light (in a sunny location outdoors) for 7 to 15 minutes. Fabric will change color during exposure and areas covered by plant material will maintain original color. The time will vary depending on the intensity of the sun. Do a test on a sample piece of material first, if you like. If using fabric and only one side of fabric is exposed, the unexposed side will remain white when it is rinsed. Flip fabric and expose both sides, for blue color on both sides. By exposing both sides, a deeper shade of indigo will be achieved than by exposing only one side. If print is underexposed, the material will be a lighter shade of blue and pattern will be faint.

4. Rinse fabric or paper in water until water runs clear. Hang paper or fabric to dry.

MATERIALS AND TOOLS

Fresh or dried plant cuttings

Plywood board to support cardboard (at least as large as piece being printed)

Sheet of corrugated cardboard (at least as large as piece being printed)

Sun print paper or fabric (see Resources)

Sewing pins, or a pane of non-UV-resistant glass

Fresh water for rinsing cyanotypes, in bowls or in a sink

NOTE

If fabric needs ironing, iron without steam since the UV treatment is water soluble and will spot if water touches it before printing.

MATERIALS AND TOOLS

Woven bamboo plywood (found online or at green hardware stores)

Quick-drying clear glue, such as Fabri-Tac

Twill tape, ¾" to 1" wide

Tin snips

Scissors

Measuring tape

Pencil

Woven bamboo plywood is typically used as a renewable resource for covering walls and ceilings, but it can also be used to create place mats bound with twill tape. The same technique works for making runners, coasters, or even a full-sized table covering for an old table that needs dressing up.

1. Using tin snips, cut woven bamboo plywood to size, approximately 14" by 18" for place mats.

2. Measure perimeter of cut piece of bamboo plywood. Cut twill tape to a length about 1" longer than perimeter.

3. Run a bead of glue along half of one edge of cut bamboo plywood and spread it out evenly with finger. Starting in the middle of one side will make it easy to reconcile the ends of the tape when the work is completed. Starting with one end of twill tape, place tape along edge with about half of width of tape on bamboo mat and the rest hanging over the edge. Press into place, making sure glue runs close to outside edge of tape to ensure that it does not peel back from plywood. If you find it easier, glue can be applied to twill tape and then pressed onto bamboo panel.

4. When you reach the corner, make a 45-degree fold to create a mitered detail at the corners. Continue to add glue and wrap the tape around all 4 sides and corners until you get all the way around the plywood piece and the ends overlap. Trim tape to size, fold under at a 45-degree angle, and glue final edge into place.

Entertaining outdoors involves a lot of carting back and forth from the kitchen, and finding ways to simplify that makes life easier. Milk bottle carriers, from the days of milkmen making deliveries, can be found easily online or at flea markets. They're great for carting out silverware and napkins (just put pint glasses in the individual compartments and fill with silverware and napkins), holding a collection of potted culinary herbs—which also make a great centerpiece—or stocked as a portable bar with alcohol and mixers. Saving one of the compartments for lemons and limes means you won't have to run inside for a garnish.

THE RANDALL BOXES
13 SPRING STREET
VERGENNES, VT 05491
(802) 877-3082

TOMATOES, CORN, AND PEPPERS

For many of us, summer begins with the first ripe tomato or freshly picked sweet corn and culminates with the ripening of the first chili and bell peppers. And, as all three originated in the Americas, it makes sense that they play such an important role at Fourth of July and Labor Day barbecues and picnics. After all, what could be a better cause for celebration than the ripening of our native bounty?

These trellises are ideal for growing fruiting vines such as tomatoes and also provide a nice architectural element in the vegetable garden. In the heat of the summer, the shade provided by the vines growing over the trellis creates a spot to start cooler-season crops, such as lettuces, so that they don't bolt in the summer sun and heat. We chose to use plastic-coated lobster pot wire, which also makes a great countertop for plant racks in a nursery or a greenhouse, since it won't rust. You can substitute metal hardware cloth or hog wire from an agricultural supply store.

The technique for building these frames is simple—think about making two picture frames and routing out the inner edge of each to hold the wire insert in place, then connecting them with a butt hinge. The hinge also allows them to fold up for easy storage during the off season against a wall in the garage or garden shed.

If you live in a windy area, anchor the A-frames in place with stakes through the base.

1. Using table saw, rip down both ⁵⁄₄" planks for a total of six 1"×1¼"×10' (nominal) strips.

2. Using miter saw, cut 4 of the 10' lengths into 6' and 4' lengths. Cut four 3' lengths out of remaining two 10' sections. The remaining material will not be used in this project.

3. Using table saw with the ¼" dado blade, cut a channel down the length of each 6' and 4' board. The channel must be ⁵⁄₈" deep and centered on the 1" side. (The wire mesh used determines the width of the channel. The wire should be a snug fit.)

4. Adjust height of dado blade to ⁷⁄₈" for a deeper channel. Apply the same cuts to each 3' board; repeat these cuts to opposite side of each 3' board. This will produce eight 3'×³⁄₈"×1½" slats from the original 4 lengths.

5. Begin to construct a "picture frame" around the wire panel. Setting miter saw blade to a 45-degree angle, cut each of the 6' lengths to 62½" from outside of the board (the nonchannel side). The inside board length (channel side) will measure 59⁵⁄₈".

6. Repeat this process with the 4' lengths, with a finish dimension of 37¹⁵⁄₁₆" length at the outside nonchannel side and 35" at the inside channel side.

[CONTINUED]

MATERIALS

One ⁵⁄₄"×8"×10' pine board (see Notes)

One ⁵⁄₄"×6"×10' pine board (see Notes)

Two 3'×5' sheets of vinyl-coated heavy-gauge lobster pot wire (1"×1" squares)

2" exterior-grade stainless steel wood screws

2½" stainless steel finish nails

Two 3" exterior-grade butt hinges

Latex stain or wood preservative/finish

TOOLS

Pencil

Tape measure

Carpenter's square

Hammer

Drill

³⁄₃₂" drill bit

Screw bit or screwdriver

Countersink bit

Table saw with standard blade

¼" dado blade

Miter saw with general-purpose blade

Palm sander

120 grit sandpaper

Red cedar can be used instead of pine: it's longer lasting and rot resistant. However, it is more expensive.

Instead of the ⁵⁄₄" planks, substitute two 10' cedar 2×4s. Rip each 2×4 down to three 1"×1¹⁄₂"×10' (nominal) lengths.

7. Sand and apply stain or finish to all the wood components, as desired.

8. Once dry, begin the assembly. Place wire panel on a flat surface and insert each side into the channel of the corresponding board lengths. Adjust corners of frame to 90 degrees using carpenter's square. When frame has taken shape, permanently secure it in place by drilling pilot holes using ³⁄₃₂" bit on each of four corners, countersinking holes, and inserting screws from outside of frame to adjoining component. Screw each side of corner to the opposing side of the frame.

9. Attach remaining slats to interior of each side of frame. Space them out equally to create 3 wire sections. Drill pilot holes on sides of frame to accept the finish nails that will hold the slats in place. These slats will lock in wire and increase stability of frames.

10. Lay the completed trellis frames end to end on a flat surface. Attach hinges to each frame 6" in from the side of frame. The trellis is now ready for use in the garden.

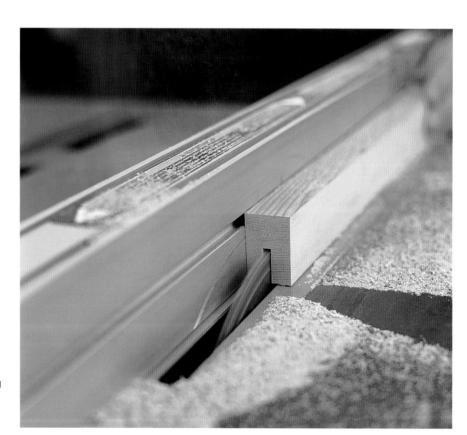

Using a dado blade to create a channel for holding lobster pot wire in place gives these A-frames a professional look with minimal fuss.

Fried green tomatoes have been a popular Southern treat for generations, but ripe tomatoes at their peak are also perfect for simply pan-frying in an old cast-iron pan on the grill. The pine nuts and Japanese bread crumbs in this recipe toast up nicely and give these delectable treats a crisp crust that makes them a perfect light lunch alongside a simple green salad.

If you fall in love with this recipe in the peak of the summer, it will also work well with the green tomatoes that remain when the tomato season comes to its inevitable end.

1. Preheat grill and griddle pan. Crack eggs into a shallow dish and beat lightly with a fork, then set aside. On a flat plate combine the bread crumbs, cheese, basil, and pine nuts. Add salt and pepper, to taste.

2. Dip the sliced tomatoes into the egg wash, then dredge through the dry mixture. Pour a small amount of oil on the griddle and place breaded tomatoes on grill. Do not overcrowd griddle; work in batches if necessary.

3. Cook tomatoes 6 to 8 minutes per side—the time will depend on the heat of the grill and ripeness of the tomato. Transfer cooked tomatoes to serving platter and continue until all the tomatoes are cooked.

4. Squeeze lemon over top of cooked tomatoes. Serve immediately.

SERVES 4

2 large eggs
1 cup panko (Japanese-style) bread crumbs
1 cup coarsely grated or shredded Parmesan
1 cup basil, roughly chopped
½ cup pine nuts
Salt and freshly ground pepper to taste
4 tomatoes, sliced ½ inch thick
Vegetable oil for griddle
1 lemon, cut in half

NOTE

Have the grill and griddle pan hot before beginning to dredge and coat tomatoes.

SAVING HEIRLOOM TOMATO SEED

MATERIALS

Ripe heirloom tomato
Pint-sized plastic container
Water
Strainer
Old window screen or paper
   plate
Labels
Coin envelopes

Without the work of gardeners around the world saving the seeds of their favorite varieties and passing them along from generation to generation, many heirloom tomatoes would have disappeared decades ago. Saving seeds from year to year is a time-honored tradition. Heirloom varieties of tomatoes (open-pollinated, nonhybrid forms that have been passed on from generation to generation) come true from seed and can be collected each season to be grown again the following year. Hybrid varieties do not come true to type and their seeds will produce tomatoes unlike those of their parent. The method is quite simple, and passing along seeds of your favorite tomato ensures that variety's existence for years to come.

Another advantage of heirloom varieties is that many of them are well suited to a particular region of the country, allowing gardeners in cool-summer areas like Seattle and the Berkshires to select tomatoes that have the best chance of ripening in their neck of the woods.

1. Take a very ripe tomato and cut it in half. Squeeze the pulp out into a pint-sized plastic container. Fill the container about 1/3 full with water.

2. Cover loosely and let container sit in a warm spot away from direct sunlight for about 2 to 3 days. A mold will form on the surface of the water. This mold will separate the pulp from the seeds.

3. Strain mold and remove any large chunks of pulp and discard. Any dead seeds will have floated to the top and should also be discarded. Take remaining liquid and pour it through a strainer.

4. Rinse seeds clean by pouring several passes of water over seeds and rinse off remaining pulp.

5. Spread out seeds on a screen, making sure to label them with the variety name. Or use a paper plate and label plate with the tomato variety name and let dry for 2 to 3 days in a dry spot out of direct sun.

6. After seeds have dried, place them in a coin envelope. Write the name of the variety on the envelope. Store envelope in a climate-controlled space in a dry airtight container. The ideal location is a dry, dark, cool spot.

MATERIALS

16-inch-diameter hanging
wire basket

Sphagnum moss (available at
craft and garden stores)

Good-quality potting soil

3 small cherry or grape
tomato plants, such as 'Sun
Gold'

2 to 3 basil plants (optional)

Hanging containers are often filled with colorful flowering plants to get in one more touch of color. But why not use a hanging wire planter to grow America's favorite homegrown vegetable, the tomato? Since tomatoes are vines, they can easily prosper in a container. And they won't even need staking, because they shouldn't be hitting the ground anytime soon.

We used this idea with grape- and cherry-sized tomatoes so that gravity didn't take its toll on the crop, and quickly found that the yellow and orange varieties of these miniature tomatoes are as pretty as any flower.

1. Line inside of basket with large sheets of sphagnum moss. Fill in gaps with smaller pieces, leaving 3 small evenly spaced openings along sides of basket.

2. Take tomato plants out of containers and feed stem of tomato plant through openings in moss-filled planter, setting the root ball inside sphagnum-lined basket. Repeat with remaining tomato plants. Do not worry about some of the stem being buried. Unlike other plants, the stems of tomatoes will not rot underground and will actually root in and give the plant a stronger root base.

3. Add potting soil to top of basket. Plant top with several basil plants, if you like. Water thoroughly and hang in a sunny spot. Rotating the basket from time to time after watering will ensure that each plant gets enough sun. Harvest tomatoes when ripe.

The patterns of nature have inspired designers and artists for centuries. Using the pattern of a cob of corn to faux-finish an unfinished piece of furniture is simple and yields beautiful results. If corn isn't available, using fern fronds yields a similarly interesting result, although they need to be pressed in place, not rolled.

This same process can be applied on paper, using nontoxic paint, to create colorful wrapping paper with your children.

MATERIALS AND TOOLS

2 colors of interior latex paint that complement each other

A piece of unfinished furniture

One ear of corn

Paintbrush

Scrap wood or paper

Paper towels

1. Choose which of the 2 paints you want to use as the base color. With brush, paint piece of unfinished furniture with base coat of interior latex paint and set aside to dry. Wash your brush. Shuck ear of corn and remove all silk.

2. Brush the second paint color onto corn cob. Leave ends of cob free of paint so cob can be rolled without getting paint on your hands. Roll cob on scrap wood or paper to get used to technique. Blot paint with a paper towel to remove any excess. Reapply paint to cob as needed and continue rolling.

3. When base coat is dry on furniture, roll cob with contrasting paint onto dry paint surface. Do this in small sections to keep the paint application even. After each roll of cob, blot the wet paint with a paper towel to remove excess paint. Allow to dry.

Farmers have long used corncribs to store feed for their livestock in a dry place with good air circulation. So what better form to mimic for a storage bin in the backyard? The open sides made of lath make it perfect for storing pool toys, cushions, life jackets, and lawn chairs that might mildew without air circulation, and taking things in and out is as easy as raising the roof. This project can be built on a smaller scale as a perfect toy bin for young children; at its present scale, it works well for the kayaking enthusiast or for pool toys.

1. Using table saw, rip down all six 2×4s to a finished dimension of 1½"×1½". These will be used as the framing studs for the corncrib.

2. Construct the floor, which will have a finished dimension of 30"×48". Take one ripped-down 8' stud and cut down to 2 equal 48" lengths. Take 2 ripped-down 10' studs and cut down into two 28½" and three 26¾" lengths. Save remainder. At either end of the 48" pieces, create a rabbet joint that will accept the 28½" lengths. The joint depth should be ¾" so that when the 28½" piece sits in joint, the finished length of either side is 30". Next, attach three 26¾" pieces evenly apart within frame to create floor supports. All framing is attached with wood glue and stainless steel screws.

3. Cut down 4x4 post to four 7" lengths. Set posts on a workbench and rest floor frame on top of 4 posts. With each post lined up at the corners, trace out the frame corner onto each post. Remove this material to a depth of 1½" with the table saw and a wood chisel. This notch will accept the frame corner so that top of post and each outer side sits flush with floor frame. Secure each post to frame with glue and stainless steel screws. Flip the base upside down and attach the feet by using the utility knife to cut out the rubber mat to size of each post bottom. Attach feet to post with stainless steel screws. Be sure to countersink screws below surface of rubber feet.

4. Next, begin construction of lower half of 4 side walls. Using two 10' ripped-down studs, cut 6 pieces to a length of 28". With the miter saw, cut each piece at a 10-degree angle on both ends. The miter cuts at both ends of stud should be parallel to each other. Attach 4 of these posts to the 4 corners so the angles tilt the posts out on 48" sides of floor frame (the posts will sit flush with 30" sides). Form an additional two 10' ripped-down studs, and cut a 39½" length piece from each. With glue and screws, fasten these pieces on corner posts so that the short sides of frame are attached across the top. Using two 8' ripped-down studs, cut a 45" length from each. Then, connect the long sides of frame together, attaching these pieces so that they sit flush inside top framing of the sidewalls. Next, attach

MATERIALS

One 2"×4"×12' cedar board

One 2"×4"×8' cedar board

Four 2"×4"×10' cedar boards

One 4"×4"×28" cedar board

Nine 5½"×10' cedar clapboards

Three 1"×6"×10' cedar boards

Four 1"×6"×8'cedar boards

8"×8"×¾" rubber matting

1½" stainless steel 4d shake nails

2½" stainless steel screws

Galvanized poultry staples

2'6"×4' piece of 14-gauge vinyl-coated wire, preferably with one-inch squares

Two 2"×¾" stainless steel butt hinges

Exterior wood glue

TOOLS

Pencil

Tape measure

Table saw

Miter saw

Hammer

1" wood chisel

Level

Drill

6 countersink drill bit

Screw bit or screw gun

Wire cutters

Utility knife

NOTE

To preserve the cedar, apply a coat of water sealant or other exterior-grade finish of choice or allow it to weather to a natural silver.

remaining 28" angled pieces on center of each of the long side walls. Using leftover studs from floor construction, cut out two 27½" pieces and attach one on center in each of short side walls.

5. With wire cutters, cut the 14-gauge wire to size for floor base. Set trimmed wire on base and hammer in galvanized poultry staples.

6. Build two ridge beam supports. From two new 10' ripped-down studs, cut two 17½" lengths and attach them vertically on top of shorter side walls, aligning them on center with the center studs of short walls. From remaining stock of 8' stud, cut one 49½" length to be used as the ridge beam. Set table saw blade at 40 degrees, align the fence ¾" out from blade, and rip a 40-degree bevel down length of both sides of ridge beam. The slope of the roof will be 40 degrees. Attach the ridge beam on top of the two 17½" pieces so that there is a ¾" overhang on both ends.

7. From one of the remaining 10' studs cut out four 19" lengths. Cut one end of each piece to have 40-degree miter cut. With the screws, attach each of these pieces to the top of the framing of side walls so that 90-degree side butts up to the bottom of the 17½" center stud on short wall and the 40-degree miter side matches slope of roof peak. Next, cut out two 22" lengths for front side roof trusses from remainder of 10' stud. One side will have a miter cut of 40 degrees, the other will have a miter cut of 50 degrees. Note that these cuts are not parallel on either end; they run opposite each other. The 22" measurement is based on the longer side of the miter cuts. Attach 40-degree mitered edge of truss 1½" below top of 17½" stud and fasten other end to top of 19" piece.

8. Next, cut out three 29½" lengths for roof trusses, making a miter cut of 40 degrees at one end of each of these. Use the screws to attach each of these trusses on the opposite side of roof flush with the ridge beam, just below the bevel. Place a truss on either end, and one on center. The bottom of these trusses will overhang the wall frame by several inches. From another 10' stud cut out two 21¾" pieces and attach them at the bottom of the trusses, in between the ends.

9. With remaining stud stock, construct door frame. Cut out one 45" length, one 47¾" length, one 26¼" length, and two 29" lengths. The two 29" lengths will have a 40-degree miter cut on one end. With the 29" lengths lying flat with the miter cut side facing down, screw in the 45" length between the two 29" pieces. Each end of the 45" length should be set back just past the miter cut. Next, attach the 47¾" length to the opposite end. Then add the 26¼" length on center between the 2 longer lengths.

10. Position door frame on top of front side of corncrib and mark out location for the 2 butt hinges. They should be placed approximately 6" in from either end. Remove door and fasten a small block 1½"×1½"×4" fashioned from leftover material beneath the ridge beam where the hinges will fasten. These blocks will allow the hinges to remain securely fastened. Attach hinges to door and ridge beam.

11. Apply exterior sheathing. Each side of the roof will require 9 clapboards cut to a length of 51". For our project we set each course 3½" apart. Attach the clapboards using 4d shake nails.

12. Rip down all seven 1×6 cedar boards to a width of 1½" slats. Each board will produce 3 widths of 1½" slats. From the 8' lengths cut 20 lengths to 48" long. Attach 10 of these to either side with screws, setting the spacing at 1½" apart. Attach each of these slats with 4d nails and wood glue. Repeat process for other 2 narrower walls, cutting each of these slats to size to match angle of walls. Ten-degree mitered cuts will be required on either end of the lower half of the slats, and 40-degree mitered cuts will be required on the upper half of side walls. The ends of these slats should also overlap the adjacent side slats already in place.

13. Using leftover material, create a prop stick and cradles to use for holding the door open. Cut a leftover slat to a length of 23 inches and drill a hole close to one end of the slat, slightly larger than the screw or nail. This hole will allow you to hang the stick from a screw or nail on the inside of the corncrib. Next, cut a 4" length of scrap stud and notch out a groove at 90 degrees to the block to allow the stick to sit inside. Attach this block to the side wall at a height just below where the roof truss begins. From a second block, notch out a piece at a 45-degree angle to the block to accept the other end of the stick. Attach this block to the top right corner of the door frame, just underneath the clapboard.

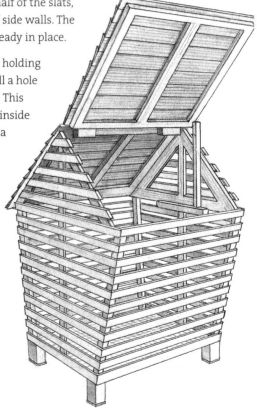

The roof is hinged
for easy access

CORNHUSK LABELS

Cornhusks can easily be recycled into houseplant labels with bamboo skewers and a bit of flexible wire. For a nice touch at a dinner party, use the labels as place cards, putting each in a small potted plant that guests can take home later. To make the labels, just press the cornhusks in a plant press, or use an iron on a high setting with a pressing cloth to dry them out quickly. Cut the husk to the desired leaflike shape and write the name of the plant with a fine-point permanent pen. Pinch one end of the husk leaf over the end of a toothpick or skewer and fasten it by twisting some wire around the base of the husk.

chile ristras and freezing, drying, and storing peppers

 It is hard to imagine world cuisine without certain vegetables. Even though peppers and chilies are native to the Americas, the cuisines of Spain, Italy, and even Thailand wouldn't be the same without these curvaceous capsicums.

Whether peppers are dried and ground into powder or transformed into a hanging *chile ristra* of the Southwest, having them on hand is a tradition well worth continuing. When we met self-professed (or confessed) chilihead Susan Belsinger, we were delighted with her ideas for keep these peppers on hand all year long—by air-drying, drying in the oven, or roasting and freezing them.

Remember that the dried chilies should not crumble into dust but should really still have some flexibility left to them.

MAKING CHILE RISTRAS

MATERIALS
Chilies, as many as desired for length of string
Twine
Rubber bands
Thread or thin wire

drying times

Small Thai	6 hours
Serrano	1 day
Santa Fe grandee	About 2 days
New Mexico or Ancho	3 to 4 days
Bell pepper	5 days

The technique for the long *ristra* with larger peppers is fine for those in a hot, dry climate, but the single-strand *ristra* (opposite) will work even for those in cooler, more humid environments. Like onion and garlic braids, *ristras* should be used from the top down.

long ristra with large fruit

1. Use strong twine that can support the final weight of the peppers. Take 3 chilies and bundle them together at the stem. Connect their stems with a rubber band.

2. Thread the bundle of 3 peppers onto twine and tie to bottom end of twine.

3. Continue making bundles and threading them onto the twine until desired length is reached.

single strand with smaller fruit such as red Thai chilies

1. Thread a chili through the flesh just under the cap onto wire or sturdy thread. Continue threading chilies until desired length is attained.

2. Hang in an indirectly lit, dry location and allow chilies to dry. Rotate *ristra* from time to time to provide even air circulation and exposure to light.

MATERIALS

Chilies
Baking sheet
Glass jars and lids

1. Set the oven to 150 degrees F.

2. Place peppers on a baking sheet so that they are not touching one another. Place in oven to dry. Drying times will vary, depending on the size and variety of the pepper (see box on page 72).

3. When peppers are free of moisture and crisp but flexible, they are ready to store. Store in glass jars or grind them into a powder to use in cooking. Ground chili powder can be stored in the freezer to maintain freshness.

ROASTING AND FREEZING PEPPERS

This method will work for a variety of peppers and chilies and is a great way to store excess bell peppers for winter use as well. The skin slips easily off the pepper after freezing, averting the time-consuming task of removing it after roasting.

1. Over the flame of a medium-hot grill or in your broiler, blacken the skin of the chili on all sides.

2. To use the pepper immediately, drop in a paper bag and let stand until cool enough to handle. Remove it from the bag and scrape skin off with a knife.

3. To freeze peppers, let them cool in paper bag, then put them in a resealable freezer bag in the freezer. When they are thawed, skin will slip right off.

HERBS

Herbs have been coveted for centuries, by gardeners and nongardeners alike, for medicinal, culinary, and spiritual purposes. Not only do the essential oils of these revered plants enhance the pleasure of eating, but their fragrance also connects us to memories of our past and to the lands from which our ancestors came. Perhaps this is why we are so inventive in finding places to grow them.

MATERIALS

Several yards twisted
    electrical copper wire
Cast-iron shelf bracket
Small pebble, preferably
    slightly flat and about 1" in
    diameter
Exterior-grade 1½" screws
    (often supplied with
    brackets)
Potted plants for hanging,
    each in a container with a
    wide lip

TOOLS

Wire cutters
Screwdriver

Great ideas come from looking at familiar objects in a new way. With the addition of some copper wire and a pebble, a readily available cast-iron shelf bracket takes on a whole new life as a plant hanger. We made a series of them, attached them to a sunny exterior wall, and created a hanging garden within a stone's throw of the outdoor kitchen. • *Photograph on page 74*

1. Figure out length you want pot to hang down from bracket. Cut a piece of wire to the sum of this length plus 10". Cut a second piece of wire twice as long as the first. Fold long piece in half.

2. Tightly twist one end of shorter wire around midpoint of long wire where it has been folded in half. Twist about ½" of the wires together.

3. Place pebble under twisted area of the wires and divide 3 strands so that the 3 wires divide pebble into 3 sections. Gather wires underneath pebble and twist together tightly on underside of stone. Stones' shapes vary, so wrapping method may need to be slightly different for each.

4. Thread the 3 ends of wire through hole at end of bracket from which the plant will hang. Trim wire ends so they are even with each other. Fold ends up about 2" to form a hook on each strand's end. Set aside.

5. Cut a length of wire about 6" longer than your herb pot's circumference just below its lip. Wrap wire around pot just below lip. Tightly cross wire over itself and pull wire back in same direction from which it came. This is to ensure that your circle is the right size to hold pot. Remove circle of wire from pot and twist excess wire ends tightly around ring to strengthen circle and secure ends.

6. Evenly space 3 hooks on ends of the wires from step 4 to ring. Twist wire hook around itself to securely fasten it to ring. Trim any excess wire and fold up piece of twisted wire neatly around stone.

7. Screw bracket to wall with exterior-grade screws. Place your herb pot in the ring.

Wrapping the top pebble

Creating the pot holder

Many people like to cook with herbs. An easy way to have fresh herbs accessible is to grow them in a container such as a strawberry pot. Provided it is sited in a sunny location, the pot can be placed right outside the kitchen door, near the grill, or by an outdoor kitchen, so that seasonings are always at hand.

An old-fashioned strawberry pot is perfect for growing herbs because its pockets allow you to grow chives, basil, thyme, mint, oregano, and rosemary in one container. Drainage is easily improved by using a paper towel tube and gravel to create a drainage column down the center. Because its roots require a substantial depth of soil in order to prosper, rosemary should be placed in the top of the container.

MATERIALS

Strawberry pot

Empty paper towel roll

Pea gravel or turkey grit

Organic soilless potting
medium

A variety of potted herbs (3-
inch containers)

Time-release fertilizer
(optional)

1. Set an empty paper towel roll upright in the center of the strawberry pot and then fill the tube with the stone or gravel, before adding soil to the container.

2. Start filling the container with potting medium. Since the herbs will be used for cooking, use an organic-based potting mix. When mix reaches the first round of holes in pot, begin setting in plants. Add time-release fertilizer, if desired, following package directions. Put taller plants like sage and chives in the lower pockets, and shorter plants like thyme and oregano in the upper pockets. Fill in around each plant with potting mix. Leaving a bit of space on the top of each planting pocket will make it easier to water the pot without water running all over the place. Top-dressing each pocket with a bit of pea stone or gravel to keep the crowns of the plants dry will also ensure that the soil does not run off when the planter is watered.

3. Once the pockets are filled, carefully tease out the cardboard roll before planting the top of the pot so that you end up with a vertical column of stone in the center of the pot.

4. Plant the topmost part of the pot with lavender or rosemary, filling in with potting mix and topping it off with pea stone or gravel.

5. Set container in a sunny location. Keep it well watered and use a water-soluble fertilizer biweekly.

Though using fresh herbs in cooking has become somewhat common, it is a hassle to have to run out to the garden every time you need a bit of sage. Fresh herbs can always be at hand with this planter box, designed to hang over a porch or deck railing. Although this design is specified to fit over a standard 2×4 railing and is locked in place by zinc half-turn buttons that secure it to the railing, it can easily be customized to fit over any size railing.

Starting with variegated and colorful forms of sage, thyme, basil, and shiso (perilla) will make for a colorful planter box and still provide you with herbs for cooking. Lining the base of the box with 1½ inches of gravel allows water to drain freely from holes drilled in bottom of planting box, making it ideally suited to growing herbs, but these planters can also be used for growing other plants, such as edible nasturtiums or scented geraniums.

If this project seems hard to visualize while working through the directions, keep in mind that it is a simple planter box with the base designed to fit a 2×4 railing within its form.

1. Using miter saw, cut one 1"×10"×10' down to 65" and 55" lengths. Next, use table saw to rip down both lengths to 7" wide. Rip another 1" width from remaining pieces.

2. Cut the 7" widths into two 42" lengths (planter sides), two 7½" lengths (planter ends), and one 7" length (middle divider). Create top trim pieces by cutting 1" widths into two 43" lengths and three 10" pieces.

3. Cut remaining 1"×10"×10' board into two 42" lengths. Rip down both 42" pieces into one 4⅞" width (bottom center board), two 2⁵⁄₁₆" widths (left and right side bottom boards), and two ⅞" widths (sides of railing slot).

4. Install 1¹⁄₁₆" dado blade on table saw and set blade to a height of ⁵⁄₁₆". Cut rabbet joints on both ends of each of the two 7"×42" sides to later accept 7½" end pieces of the box.

5. Set dado blade height to ⅞". Using repeated strokes of the dado blade, create a 3⁹⁄₁₆"-wide notch in center of bottom edge of both 7½" end pieces. This will create the channel in which the porch or deck railing will sit.

6. Dry-fit these 4 pieces of the planter box by inserting end pieces into rabbets on side pieces. Predrill and countersink holes for screwing sides and ends together. Disassemble box, apply glue, reassemble, insert #7 screws, and clamp to dry.

[CONTINUED]

MATERIALS

Two 1"×10"×10' redwood boards (1¹⁄₁₆" thick)

#7 stainless steel screws, 1⁵⁄₈" long

Exterior wood glue

4 half-turn buttons (zinc)

#8 stainless steel screws, ½" long

Teak oil

TOOLS

Pencil

Table saw with ripping blade

1¹⁄₁₆" dado blade

Miter saw with finish blade

Drill

Countersink drill bit

⅜" drill bit

Screw bit or screw gun

Framing square

Tape measure

Two 36" Quick-Grip clamps

Palm sander

Fine-grade sandpaper

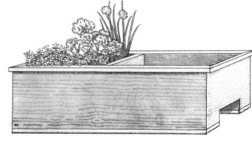

The middle divider helps separate your herbs

7. Set dado blade height to $1^9/_{16}$". Using repeated strokes of the dado blade, create a $4^7/_8$" notch in center of bottom edge of 7" middle divider.

8. Dry-fit middle divider; predrill and countersink holes for securing divider with screws. Apply glue, clamp, and attach together with #7 screws.

9. Cut the $4^7/_8$" bottom center board to a length of $40^{11}/_{16}$"; fit into notch of middle divider and align bottom edge flush with top edge of notches on box ends.

10. Predrill, countersink, and attach bottom center board through sides with #7 screws. Also secure up through underside into middle divider.

11. Using #7 screws, attach the left side bottom board and right side bottom boards (both $2^5/_{16}$"×42") and attach the 2 sides of the railing slot (both $^7/_8$"×$40^5/_8$") to the underside of the bottom center board and the edge of the bottom side boards. Drill out six $^3/_8$" drainage holes through the bottom side pieces, setting holes at an equal distance from one another. Predrill holes on drainage strip, 4 inches in from each side. Using #8 screws, attach turn buttons so they can turn and lock planter onto rail. Hand-tighten.

12. Cut top trim pieces to size, miter corners, and attach to top edge of planter box using only exterior wood glue. Trim should overhang outside face of planter box by $^1/_4$". Clamp in place to dry.

13. Lightly sand and apply teak oil to the exterior.

The flavor of fresh herbs is incomparable, but having access to your own freshly dried herbs or even to a bit of frozen basil ensures a cook's ability to make tasty meals whatever the season.

Drying herbs from the garden and properly storing them allows the flavors of the garden to be with us year-round. It is best to replace dried herbs every year, so why not make an annual harvest of your herbs?

TO DRY HERBS

Harvest perennial herbs no later than about ten weeks before first frost, in order to give plants time to harden off before winter. Water herbs well the day before harvesting. Cut back perennial herbs such as rosemary, sage, thyme, and oregano by about two-thirds. Set cut branches on a screen, or hang in small bunches, to dry in a cool, dry place out of direct sunlight. The herbs are completely dry once a piece crackles when crumbled between your fingers. This usually takes between a few days and several weeks. Once dry, place whole leaves in clean jars and store in cool, dry, dark place. Do not break up leaves until using herbs, because doing so releases their essential oils.

Some herbs—for instance, oregano, rosemary, and the leaves of dill and cilantro—dry well in the refrigerator. Simply make sure they are free of any water on stems or leaves and place in brown paper lunch bags. Set closed bags upright on refrigerator shelf; turn daily until dry, shaking bags to ensure air circulation around leaves. They will dry in several weeks and can then be stored as above.

TO FREEZE BASIL AND PARSLEY

Basil is one herb that does not dry well and is best used fresh. But its fresh, open taste is wonderful in the winter, calling summer to mind. The best way to store basil for off-season use is to chop it and add it to olive oil. Then, by placing a cupful in a resealable plastic freezer bag and pressing it down into a thin layer the size of the bag and sealing it, it can be frozen and broken off in chunks for adding to soups and sauces, or defrosted and used for pesto. As the garlic, nuts, and cheese in pesto do not take well to freezing, simply pulling out a piece of the frozen basil and adding it to the remaining ingredients will create the best-tasting pesto in the off season. Parsley can be stored in a similar manner.

STONE

Formed from aggregates of minerals by the forces of nature, stone has a sense of permanence that helps ground our lives and lets us put our mark on the world around us. Whether carved to commemorate the planting of a tree, used as an edging in the border, or re-formed into planting troughs for alpines and conifers, stone gives our gardens and homes a rock-solid foundation on which to continue to build our world.

STONE TREE MARKER

MATERIALS AND TOOLS

Pencil

Assorted stone-grinding
  silicon-carbide bits for
  rotary tool, including one
  with a sharp point for
  lettering

Rotary grinding tool, such as a
  Dremel (see Notes)

1 stone or a slate tile, plus
  extras for testing (see
  Notes)

Safety glasses

NOTES

Do not use the cordless
  variety of rotary tool for
  this project—its motor is
  not as strong.

Stone varies in hardness;
  softer stones such as
  soapstone, slate, and
  alabaster are easier to
  carve.

 Whether planting a tree as a gift for a friend, to commemorate the birth of a child, or for another special event, a stone tree marker is a wonderful way to memorialize the occasion. Set the stone at the base of tree when planting; as the tree matures the stone will settle into place, marking the occasion for years to come. This idea originated when we visited the Swarthmore Arboretum in Pennsylvania and saw a beautiful carved stone acorn inscribed with the planting date of a majestic 100-year-old oak.

While the artistry involved in carving a stone acorn that can then be nestled among the trees roots may be beyond the average do-it-yourselfer, a rotary tool with stone-cutting bits enables even a novice to create these commemorative markers. Once the tool has been mastered, you can not only carve stone labels for trees and plants in the garden but also easily personalize terra-cotta pots and engrave slate panels with address numbers with relative ease. Of course, it is important to wear safety glasses to prevent injury, but they just make you look more like a professional stone carver. • *Photograph on page 82*

1. Using pencil, draw initials and/or date on stone.

2. Put selected bit on grinding tool. Wearing safety glasses, start motor, and hold in a manner similar to how you would hold a pencil. Practice on an extra stone first, if you like.

3. Lightly trace over inscription with grinding bit to create a groove. On next pass, use groove to guide bit deeper. Keep making passes in grooves until desired depth and thickness are obtained.

MATERIALS

One 1"×6"×3' red cedar board
One 2"×4"×5' red cedar board
One 12"×12" piece of slate, ³/₄ inch thick (see Notes)
1¹/₂" and 2" stainless steel screws
Exterior wood glue
Cedar plugs (made out of scrap 1"-thick cedar)
Teak oil (optional)

TOOLS

Pencil
Tape measure
Drill
Countersink drill bit to match screw size
Screw bit for drill or screw gun
Plug cutter to match countersink size
Table saw
Miter saw
Coping saw
Palm sander
Fine-grade sandpaper
Four 36" bar clamps

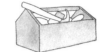

This stone-topped table will find so many uses on your terrace or porch that it may be worth creating an assembly line to make them by the dozen. Put one next to a settee or chaise longue to cradle a drink and a book. You can also build them at various heights to house a collection of plants.

Like an old stone wall, the stone top takes a beating and just looks better for the wear as it develops a patina.

1. Using a table saw, rip 1"×6" red cedar board into two lengths 1⁵/₈" wide, and two lengths ³/₄" wide. Rip 2"×4" into two 1¹/₂"×1¹/₂" posts.

2. Lay piece of slate flat on work surface and frame out perimeter of the slate with the ³/₄" stock. The wood framing should be snug but still allow slate to be removed. The corners are joined using simple butt joints (miter joints are likely

to split when screwed together). Two sides opposite each other should be same length, with shorter but equal lengths on other sides of frame.

3. Using countersink drill bit, drill pilot holes at each end of outer length of longer trim boards into shorter pieces of frame. Add a dab of wood glue and fasten with 1½" stainless steel screws. Remove slate from the frame.

4. Cut four 15¼" legs from 1½" posts. With frame on edge of a flat surface, attach each leg to frame so that outer edge of leg is flush with outside of frame. This will leave a section on interior of frame where leg is exposed and on which the slate top will rest. Drill countersink pilot holes from above, drilling into ends of 2 longer lengths of trim, being sure to offset from position of 1½" screws fastening corners. Add glue to top of leg and fasten with 2" stainless steel screws.

5. Stand table upright once all 4 legs have been attached. Measure for each cross brace between the top of 2 legs for that side. Cut brace to size from 1½"×1½" posts, and drill pilot holes at each end of underside of brace at a 45-degree angle. Add glue to the ends, position into place, and clamp brace to hold in place. Attach lower shelf base 3" from the bottom of each leg, fastening with 2" stainless steel screws. Repeat on remaining 3 sides.

6. Measure, cut, and place a ¾" trim piece on 2 interior sides of braces, on braces opposite each other. These will frame the slats for bottom shelf.

7. Measure and cut 6 shelf slats out of 1⅝" stock. The 2 slats that will sit directly on the shelf brace will need to be ripped down to a width of 1½". Attach these 2 slats from underside. Use 1½" screws with a countersink pilot hole.

8. Space the remaining slats evenly apart. Connect the slats from sides of the ¾" trim, fastening the slats to the trim using 1½" stainless steel screws. Attach shelf to base from underside, drilling into ¾" trim pieces.

9. Cut plugs for the noticeable screw holes, glue in place, trim with coping saw, and sand flush.

10. To further protect cedar and intensify appearance of wood grain, apply a couple coats of teak oil, if you like.

NOTES

Since we used a stone top that was 12" square, all measurements are dictated by dimensions for the stone top and will need to be adjusted if you select another size for the top.

Other stone tile or even ceramic tile can be substituted for the slate, but be sure the material is strong enough to support whatever weight will be placed on the table.

The bottom shelf is ideal for storing magazines

Pebble mosaic pots are a charming, rustic addition to any outdoor patio, and they are easy to make. Once the technique is mastered, which shouldn't take long, think about what else you might want to dress up in this fun fashion. The trick to making these containers look their best is to choose stones that blend together well (or contrast with one another) before beginning to adhere them to the pot, and to select a grout in a color that complements the stones. Selecting pebbles with a relatively smooth rounded finish makes it easier to wipe excess grout away from the pot.

These containers look great planted with beach grasses, which seem to dance in the wind above their pebbly pots.

1. Rinse pebbles and flowerpot to remove any dirt and dust from surface. Allow to dry.

2. Working in small sections, apply adhesive caulk to pot, moving tube tip back and forth to create an even layer. Thickness of layer of caulk will depend on size of stones—it should be thick enough to hold the stones in place but not so thick that they slide off the pot. The caulk sets relatively quickly, so start with a small patch or try first on a test surface.

3. Press stones into caulk one at a time, continuing to add new sections until the entire exterior of pot is covered. Carefully apply caulk to upper lip of pot and inside of rim and apply pebbles to first inch of interior of pot as well. Set the pot aside to dry. Caulk will be fully set in 12 to 48 hours, depending on climate and thickness of layer of caulk.

4. Use a premixed tile adhesive grout to create an additional bond with the stones. Put latex gloves on and have a bucket of water handy. Using your hands and fingers or spreading tool, spread grout onto pot. Press grout firmly into crevices between stones.

5. When pot is covered, wet sponge and wring it out. Gently wipe away excess grout with rags. Remove leftover grout smudged on stones by soaking sponge with water and squeezing it over the pot. The gentle flow of water will remove grout from surface of stones but won't disturb grout between stones. Let the pot set for 48 to 72 hours, then plant the pot.

MATERIALS

(amounts will vary depending on size of pot)
Terra-cotta flowerpot
Pebbles
Clear-grade vinyl adhesive caulk
Premixed tile adhesive grout, exterior grade if possible

TOOLS

Spreading tool for grout (optional)
Sponge
Clean rags
Bucket of water
Latex gloves

LEFT Planting Troughs with Dwarf Conifers (page 92)

RIGHT Hypertufa Nursery Pots (page 93)

Hypertufa is an artificial stone the porousness of which makes it a wonderful container for plants. These troughs, which are ideal for planting with conifers or rock garden plants, can be made in a variety of shapes and sizes. We include two methods for making these great containers. The first method simply repurposes leftover nursery pots from the garden center as the form for your trough. The greatest surprise of all is the inherent beauty of many of these everyday plastic containers once they are cast in hypertufa—and we find that they make the perfect home for small cacti. The second method begins with fashioning a shape out of nails and Styrofoam boards, allowing you to build larger troughs for planting miniature gardens. Because of their size, these require more reinforcement, support, and curing time than the first method, which we find to be the perfect project to do with friends or children.

PLANTING TROUGHS WITH DWARF CONIFERS

Dwarf conifers are slow-growing varieties that typically stay under 2 to 3 feet tall, especially if they are grown in the confined space of a hypertufa trough. With the right selection of conifers and some simple care, you can grow your own containerized miniature conifer forest in your backyard. • *Photograph on page 90*

some suggested conifers

DWARF HINOKI CYPRESS
 (Chamaecyparis obtuse)
 'Golden Sprite'
DWARF ALBERTA SPRUCE
 (Picea glauca)
MUGO PINE *(Pinus mugo)*
DWARF CHINESE FIR
 (Cunninghamia konishii) 'Little Leo'
DWARF JAPANESE CEDAR
 (Cryptomeria japonica) 'Tansu'

1. Select a hypertufa trough, making sure there is a hole in the bottom of the trough to allow drainage of excess water. A trough about 2 feet long and 16 inches wide can hold about 3 to 5 dwarf conifers.

2. Cut a piece of fiberglass screen to fit in the bottom of the trough to prevent the drainage hole from getting clogged.

3. Mix together 5 parts all-purpose potting soil with 1 part of pea gravel. The gravel will help to ensure good drainage, which is essential for most conifers.

4. Plant a selection of dwarf conifers. Select conifers with contrasting shapes and foliage to give the planting maximum impact. Plant conifers so that the crown of the plant is above the line of the soil.

5. Add stones and driftwood for a natural look, if you like.

6. Add moss on the top.

7. Water the planting and keep the trough evenly moist throughout the season.

These small hypertufa pots are just the thing for displaying succulents and other small plants. This is a good project to do with kids, but mix up the mortar before calling them to the table to do their handiwork, and make sure they join you in wearing gloves (the lime from cement can burn skin).

Repurposing plastic nursery pots as prebuilt molds for hypertufa pots makes for an easier project than building your own from scratch. Because the pots are smaller than a hypertufa trough, you don't have to add the polypropylene fibers that help strengthen larger hypertufa containers. Drainage is also easier: you make drainage holes by simply pushing a finger or dowel through the existing hole on the bottom of the pot. When selecting a plastic pot, remember that the finished container will be about 1½ inches smaller than the original, due to the thickness of hypertufa walls. • *Photograph on page 91*

MATERIALS
Perlite
Peat moss
Portland cement
Water
An assortment of plastic
  nursery pots
Cement pigment (optional)

TOOLS
Drop cloth
Plastic tub (for mixing
  ingredients)
Dust mask
Gloves
Plastic bag
Rasp (optional)
Small wooden dowel
  (optional)

1. Lay out a drop cloth to protect the work area. Wearing a dust mask and gloves, mix 3 parts perlite, 3 parts peat moss, and 2 parts Portland cement in a plastic tub. Avoid breathing any cement dust.

2. Add enough water to form a hypertufa mixture that has the consistency of moist cottage cheese. The mixture will appear darker in this form than when it dries. Pigment can be added to mixture, if desired.

3. Take a handful of wet hypertufa mixture and push it firmly against the bottom of a plastic container. Once base is about 1 inch thick, begin building the sides, pushing mixture firmly against the sides of the container to create sides that are about ¾ inch thick. Continue until rim of plastic pot is reached. Press the bottom and the sides firmly to remove air pockets.

4. Create a drainage hole by pushing your finger or small dowel through the bottom hole in the plastic pot so it penetrates the hypertufa mixture.

5. Cover the pot with a plastic bag so it remains moist while the hypertufa cures. Let the hypertufa cure for about 7 to 10 days. Once it has set, make a cut in the plastic pot so it can be torn away from the partially cured hypertufa pot.

6. If desired, use a rasp to rough up the surface of the hypertufa for a more rustic appearance.

7. Continue to let the hypertufa dry slowly for several more weeks under plastic, then remove it from the plastic and let the drying process complete in the open air. A total drying time of 3 weeks should be sufficient.

8. If a crack or pit ever develops, repair it by applying a new batch of cement to the damaged area.

LARGE HYPERTUFA TROUGHS

MATERIALS

(amounts will vary depending on size of trough)

1½" foam insulation or Styrofoam board

16d nails, 3½" long

Duct tape

Sheet of 4-mil-thick plastic, large enough to wrap trough

2"-thick plastic drain cover

Portland cement

Peat moss

Perlite

Polypropylene fibers (nylon or acrylic fibers can be substituted)

Cement pigment (optional)

1 cup liquid acrylic

Wate

TOOLS

Pencil

Tape measure

Straightedge

Utility knife

Dust mask

Gloves

Shovel

Wheelbarrow or other mixing container

Small butane torch or lighter

NOTE

Always wear rubber gloves and a mask when mixing cement. Liquid acrylic and polypropylene fibers can be found at craft or big box stores, or online.

1. Using a straightedge and knife, score and cut or break four pieces of Styrofoam insulation board to create a square or rectangular frame to your desired trough size. Connect the ends of each board by simply pushing the 16d nails through the ends of the boards where they meet at a 90-degree angle. Reinforce the frame by wrapping duct tape horizontally around it several times.

2. Place a piece of insulation board that is larger than the frame's footprint on your work surface. Lay a 4-mil sheet of plastic on top of the foam board and then set the frame on top of the plastic. The plastic must be large enough to wrap around the frame of the trough when you are finished making it.

3. Begin mixing the hypertufa. Using a wheelbarrow or other large container, add the following ingredients in a 3:4:5 ratio (actual amounts of material used will vary based on trough size): 3 parts Portland cement, 4 parts peat moss (peat must be clump free), 5 parts perlite. *Caution:* It is essential to wear gloves and a mask from this point on.

4. When the hypertufa ingredients are mixed, add a handful of polypropylene fibers (separate the fibers as much as possible), a small amount of cement coloring, if desired (adjust the quantity of coloring based on the desired finished look), and 1 cup liquid acrylic. Mix thoroughly with cement peat mixture.

5. Slowly add water to hold the mix together, being careful not to hydrate the mixture too much. The consistency of the mixture should allow you to compress a handful together, ensuring that it holds its shape. Once the right consistency is achieved, you can begin building the trough.

6. Set the plastic drain cover in the center of the trough frame and construct the trough base by packing and compressing the mixture as tightly as possible to the height of the drain cover. Proceed with building up the sidewalls by compressing the mixture in two directions, down and against the wall.

7. After completing the trough, tightly wrap the entire frame in the plastic and allow to cure for at least 24 hours and up to 7 days. Carefully unwrap after the initial curing time and remove the foam walls of the frame.

8. To provide a weathered or more natural look for the exterior, round edges of the trough with a utility knife, being careful not to remove too much material. If you like, lightly scrape sides of container for a weatherworn look. Rewrap the trough in the plastic and let set an additional 28 days to fully cure. Remove from the plastic wrap and, using a flame, melt any polypropylene fibers that are noticeable. Plant as desired.

STONE EDGING

Creating a border around a perennial bed is like putting a frame around a painting—it provides a foil to the garden and is the finishing touch that completes the picture. To put this river rock border together, just set rounded river rock in a 1-foot wide-angled frame around the border. Though it can be set simply over soil, setting it on a bed of gravel topped with stone dust will prevent it from heaving and settling as the soil expands and contracts from season to season and will help to suppress weed growth. Tapping the rocks into place with a rubber mallet helps lock them in place.

FLORA

The plant kingdom provides us with endless wonder for
the natural world. Whether it is the scent and form of an
old rose, the delicate blooms of miniature orchids, or the
variegated leaves of a succulent agave, we are drawn in
by nature's evocative beauty and given an opportunity to
slow down and take it in more closely.

MATERIALS

Three 2"×4"×12' pine boards

3½" and 2" exterior-grade
   wood screws

Eight 1"×8"×10' pine boards

One 1"×10"×8' pine board

One 2"×4"×8' pine board

Three 2"×4"×10' pine boards

TOOLS

Table saw

Miter

Drill

Screwdriver

Tape measure

Level

Framing square

Pencil

 Bringing favorite houseplants out for the season is an age-old tradition. This lath-roofed bench is ideal for providing these plants with the right amount of light and shade, whether you are an orchid enthusiast, a fernaholic, or a begonia obsessive. With its generous shelves and sturdy A-frame structure, this bench will provide shelter for any beloved houseplant collection—for example, it's a great way to care for and display your orchids. This project is made from true or dimensional lumber, so a 2x4 has the actual dimensions of 2"×4". Rough-cut pine gives this a rustic look. • *Photograph on page 96*

1. Build the four end legs of the A-frame. The finished length of the legs will be 65". To create the bottom end of the "A" leg (i.e., the end that will rest on the ground), set your miter saw to 25 degrees, lay one of the 2"×4"×12' boards flat on the saw table, and make the cut (which will result in a 65-degree angle). To make the top end (which will be a 35-degree angle), place the butt end of board against the fence (i.e., so that the board is perpendicular to the fence) and make the cut with the miter still set to 25 degrees.

2. Position two of the top ends of the "A" legs together and fasten them with 3½" screws.

3. Use the table saw to rip three 2" boards from a 1"×8"×10'. To create the 6 shelf supports (i.e., the cross bars of the "A"), use the miter saw to cut the 2" boards into two lengths of 70¼", two 55", and two 40".

4. Attach shelf supports to each "A". Position longest support 8" from the bottom; place second support 14½" up from the lower support and the third 14½" from the second. When the two "A"s are ultimately joined together, the shelf supports will be on the outside edges of the frame.

5. Next, create and attach a support for cross braces that will be installed after 2 ends of bench are joined together. Cut 2 short 1"×4" boards (ripped from pieces of 1"×8"×10'), the exact lengths of which will be determined by the specific location near the top of the "A" that you ultimately attach to the supports. Position the supports high enough on the "A"s so that they will be hidden by the 10" face board that will be installed next. Both ends of the supports will need to be angled to match the slope of the "A" legs. Attach with 2" screws.

6. Join together 2 ends of bench with a board at top of structure that runs horizontally between the 2 ends and is affixed on the plane of the "A" legs . To do so, cut 1"×10"×8' into two 4' sections and use them to join together the 2 "A" frames, on both sides of the bench.

7. From three 1"×8"×10' boards, cut 6 shelves to a length of 50"×8" and attach them to shelf supports with 2" screws.

8. Next, install 2 cross braces to stabilize the frame of bench; these will form an "X" in center of bench, between the two "A" sides. Measure the distances between cross-brace support at top of one "A" side to lowest shelf support on other "A" side. Cut the remaining 2"×4"×12' to length, with a 45-degree angle on both ends (the angled cuts will be parallel to each other). Overlap cross braces in the center of the "A" frame, wedged above the bottom shelf support and top side support. Ensure that the bench structure is square and fasten the ends with 3½" screws. Fasten the center of the "X" with 3½" screws as well.

9. To create upright supports for the structure, cut 2 of the 2"×4"×10' boards to a length of 76" and attach them with 3½" screws vertically to the center of both sides of the bench. The bottom of each support should be flush with the bottom shelf support.

10. Cut the 2"×4"×8' to 7' and the last 2"×4"×10' to 52". Rip both down to two 2×2s and build a square frame for the shade laths. Finished, the size of the frame will be 52"×88". Attach the shade frame to the top of the 2 uprights.

11. From the remaining 2×4 scraps measure and cut 4 corner braces to support the shade frame against the uprights. Angle the ends of each corner brace 45 degrees. Attach the corner braces.

12. Rip and cut the remaining 1"×8" pieces into 26 laths 1"×1¾"×52", space them 1½" apart on the shade frame, and attach each using the 2" screws.

Many orchids are epiphytic, meaning that they grow in the crooks of trees, up in the canopy above the forest floor, training their pollinators to look up for their beautiful exotic flowers. So why not grow them in the manner in which they were meant to be grown?

Marguerite Webb, from J and L Orchids in Easton, Connecticut, taught us a simple technique for mounting miniature orchids. Once they're hung from the wall, a plant rack, cylinder of hardware cloth, or even a shower rod, you will finally be seeing these orchids as they were meant to be seen. There are hundreds of miniature varieties with flower spikes less than six inches tall, so finding room for dozens of them is possible for even the most space-challenged orchid lover.

Different varieties of orchid are best suited for mounting on pieces of natural cork or on tree fern bark—consult the lists on the right. Care is relatively simple but does vary from species to species.

Grow mounted orchids indoors in cooler climates, although these orchids can go outside when danger of frost is passed (temperatures should be above 48 degrees F. at night). Choose a protected area such as a porch or in the shade of a tree where squirrels won't be likely to pilfer your precious little plants. A 10- to 15-degree drop from daytime to nighttime temperatures triggers blooms.

1. Take a small amount of sphagnum moss and pad the orchid's pseudobulbs with the moss. Place the orchid against one side of the mount (this will be cork or tree fern, depending on the variety of orchid). Gently attach moss and orchid to the mount by wrapping an 18-inch piece of fishing line several times around the orchid and moss, then wrap fishing line around the mount and tie orchid securely to mount. Trim excess fishing line with scissors.

2. Cut a piece of 16-gauge wire and bend into an S-hook for hanging orchid. Attach to back side of mount by pushing one end of S-hook into the mount. If you wish, attach a label.

3. The orchid should begin forming new roots in a few weeks and will eventually attach itself to the mount, at which time the fishing line can be cut away.

MATERIALS AND TOOLS

Sphagnum moss

Orchid

One 6-inch piece of natural cork (for orchids that prefer to dry out between waterings) or tree fern (for orchids that want to retain moisture), available through garden centers and orchid specialists

Monofilament fishing line

16-gauge wire

Wire cutters

Scissors

Labels (optional)

miniature orchids for mounting on cork

Aerangis biloba

Angraecum didieri

Dendrobium bellatulum

Dendrobium toressae

Sophronitis cernua

miniature orchids for mounting on tree fern

Barbosella cogniauxiana

Cirrhopetalum tingabarinum

Isabelia pulchella

Epidendrum porpax

Scaphosepalum rapax

MATERIALS

1 box, cedar closet-lining
    (¼" thick, 4" wide) planks
    (makes 3 to 6 boxes,
    depending on size)
3' of 6-gauge copper wire
    (straight, not coiled)
Copper brads

TOOLS

Table saw
Miter saw
Pencil
Drill
Drill bit slightly larger in
    diameter than the wire
Needlenose pliers
Wire cutters

Vanda orchids are traditionally grown in hanging boxes made of cedar, redwood, or teak slats, without any planting medium. Their roots grow through the slats in the box and attach to the box itself as they would to a tree if they were growing in the wild. Even though these boxes are designed for growing vandas, they work wonderfully for growing other epiphytic orchids or as cachepots for other plants. The cedar planks sold at many closet organizing shops are an ideal and affordable source of wood for this project, and leftover trim pieces can be used in your closet to protect sweaters from moths.

Building this box involves a process that is a cross between stringing beads on a wire and building a simple form with Lincoln Logs, and the end result looks like a good game of Jenga.

1. Cut the cedar planks to ¾"-wide strips on a table saw.

2. Decide the size of the box. Using a miter saw, cut the strips into equal lengths 1½" longer than the finished interior dimension of the box.

3. Create a jig for drilling holes in cedar strips. Make a mark on each end of the strip ⅜" from narrow end of strip and centered between the 2 long sides. Drill a hole on mark, using a bit slightly larger than the copper wire. If drilling on a worktable, set a board underneath so as not to damage work surface when drilling strips. Repeat on opposite end of strip. Use this strip as a jig or template to drill matching holes in all the other cedar strips.

4. Lay out 4 cedar strips in a square on work surface, placing them so that adjacent sides are stacked on top of one another and drilled holes line up, as if building with Lincoln Logs. Then set a series of strips between top layer to create base, spacing the strips so that the gaps between them are even.

5. Use copper brads to attach the cedar strips between the two end pieces to the base below. Do not attach either end piece, as they will be held in place by a length of copper wire.

6. Cut a length of wire about 3" longer than the desired height of the orchid box. Bend the end of the wire over ½" to a 90-degree angle. Slide the unbent end of wire through the underside of the 2 horizontal cedar strips (from step 4). Set the structure on your work surface with the long wires pointing up.

7. Slide 2 strips parallel to each other onto the wires in an alternating pattern—2 pieces along the length of the box, 2 pieces along the width—until desired height is reached.

8. Use needlenose pliers to bend and curl the end of the wire that protrudes from the top of the box into a tight coil.

9. Hang the box from the 4 wire coils with twine and plant a vanda orchid directly in box or use it as a tabletop display box for orchids or other plants by lining it with sheet moss (a liner pot can be set inside, if desired).

ROSE CUTTINGS

MATERIALS

Pruning shears

Rooting hormone (optional)

Pencil

Six 1-quart mason jars

Propagating roses from cuttings is an age-old tradition. With a simple mason jar, it is easy to turn cuttings of some of your favorite roses into new plants. Although they can be rooted at any time of year, it is best to take rose cuttings in cool weather (for people in the North, spring or early fall is best). As with any propagation method, this one is not foolproof, but it will work about three times out of four. Roses grown in this manner are own-root roses, which means they will not revert to the rootstock they are grafted onto, as can happen with many hybrid teas.

1. Cut off stems that are 6 to 8 inches tall. Cut base with pruning shears at a 45-degree angle. The tips or stems of roses that recently bloomed are easiest to root. The roses should be used as soon as possible after cutting. If bringing from another location, store in moistened paper towels in a cooler containing ice and water.

2. Remove any flowers or hips from cutting and foliage from the bottom half of the cutting. Dip the bottom 2 inches of the cutting in rooting hormone and tap off excess hormone. (This rooting hormone is optional but should increase success rate of cuttings in taking root.)

3. Select a shady place in the garden with good soil for setting in cuttings. Use a pencil as a dibble to create an impression in the soil about 2 inches deep. Put rose cutting into hole created by pencil and firm soil gently around stem with hands; water in well.

4. Set mason jar over each cutting to increase moisture. Keep soil evenly moist. Slowly, the cutting will root.

5. After a month, remove jar and give cutting a gentle tug. If it holds, it is rooted. In that case, take away jar and continue to water and care for cutting. If not, check again every week or so. After a year or so, the cutting can be transplanted.

PROPAGATING BEGONIAS

Although begonias can be propagated by vegetative cuttings, leaf cuttings, tissue culture, and from seed, the easiest way to propagate them is by vegetative cutting. Simply cut off a leaf and stem and stick cut stem end into sterile seed-starting mix or perlite. To protect cutting from drying out and to create a low-stress environment that retains moisture, place the entire pot and cutting inside a resealable plastic bag. The cutting should begin to root in about a week. As roots develop, remove plant from plastic bag and pot up as plant grows on. Allow plant to dry slightly between waterings to avoid root disease.

Climbing roses are very popular among rose enthusiasts. Despite their name, climbing roses actually do not climb at all but, rather, are trained to grow up a structure. A distinctive trellis is a great backdrop for these all-American favorites and adds an architectural element to the garden. This trellis is also ideal for other twining climbers, or it can be planted with a combination of roses and clematis.

Anyone with basic carpentry skills should be able to build this trellis, which uses materials readily available from a local home improvement center. The height of the central post and the width of the horizontal arms coming out from opposite sides of the post can easily be adjusted to suit the scale of any garden setting. An old finial from a salvage yard will top off this fanciful trellis with period style.

Since cedar is such a weather-resistant wood, it is a good choice for the central post of the trellis. The arms are hardwood dowels that come in standard lengths at your home improvement center, hardware store, or lumberyard, but cedar can be used if the trellis is going to be left in its natural state.

1. Using a chop saw, cut the 4×4 post to a length of 7'6".

2. Using your combination square and tape measure, mark the 7 arm locations lengthwise on the 2 opposite sides of the post. Marking on the center of the post, the arms are located 6", 13", 20", 27", 34", 41", and 48" from the top.

3. Using the drill press and 1" Forstner drill bit, drill holes 1½" deep at each of the 14 points. Use a level to ensure that the post is flat on the table of the drill press so that the drilled holes will be exactly perpendicular to the post face.

4. Cut the doweling to the following lengths: four 11" lengths, four 13" lengths, four 16" lengths, and two 18" lengths.

5. Glue and insert the dowels into one side of the post, smallest to largest and back to smallest again. Make sure that the dowels are perpendicular to the post.

6. Glue button-style dowel caps on the ends of the dowels. Predrill a nail hole through each cap and into the end of the dowels. Secure each dowel cap with a finish nail, using a nail set to sink each nail.

7. Allow the glue to dry thoroughly. Repeat steps 5 and 6 on the other side of the post.

[CONTINUED]

MATERIALS

One 4"×4"×8' cedar post

17' of 1" doweling, in lengths suitable for producing the set of arm lengths below (more may be needed to account for scraps)

14 wooden button-style dowel caps

1 wooden finial, scaled to fit top

2½" finish nails

Double-ended 3½" wood screw

Exterior wood glue and artist's brush

Wood putty

Primer

Paint

Cement or gravel and stone dust

TOOLS

Chop saw

Miter saw

Drill press

1" Forstner drill bit

Drill and ⅙" bit

Tape measure

Level

Combination square

Pencil

Hammer

Nail set

Putty knife

Palm sander

Fine-grade sandpaper

Post hole digger

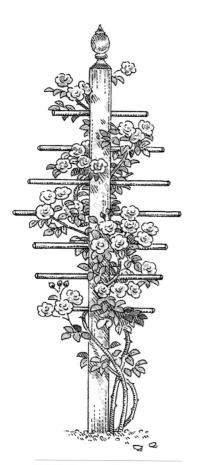

Detail of rose trellis

8. To strengthen the arms of the trellis, predrill 2 nail holes on the back side of the trellis post into each dowel and secure the arms with finish nails. Use a nail set to sink the nails.

9. Drill a hole in the center of the top of the post and the bottom of the finial, insert a double-ended screw into the post, and screw on the finial.

10. Fill each nail hole with wood putty, smooth with putty knife or finger, and sand flush.

11. Prime and paint trellis. Use a post hole digger to set trellis in ground. It can be set in cement or packed in with gravel and stone dust.

Recycled-glass mulch (see Resources) comes in a variety of colors, shapes, and sizes—some of it is tumbled more heavily. Whether it is highly polished or rougher in its finish, glass mulch adds luster and style to a potted plant or even to an entire border. It also works well as a mulch on houseplants or at the bottom of a water feature, where it will sparkle and glow.

The architectural forms of potted agaves perfectly complement the modern sensibility of the glass mulch when it's used as topdressing. Agaves prefer well-drained soil. To make your own potting mix, combine 1 part sand, 1 part turkey grit, and 1 part potting soil.

Many agaves are hardy much farther north than people imagine. They can also be kept on a cool glassed-in porch over the winter, provided they are not overwatered.

MATERIALS

Ten 8' Tonkin bamboo poles, 1" in diameter
15 to 20' of 16-gauge copper or brass wire, or raffia
2 pieces of 2'×¾" rebar
⅝" exterior-grade wood screws

TOOLS

Pencil
Aviation safety wire pliers, or standard locking pliers
Miter saw or handsaw
Framing square
Tape measure
Drill
⅜" brad point drill bit for predrilling holes
Screwdriver
¾" paddle bit
5-pound hammer or mallet

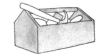 Known for its tensile strength and exotic look, bamboo is ideally suited to creating trellises for scrambling vines. When the plants are in full form, this trellis can block an unsightly view. Even early in the season, the structure itself holds appeal as a garden ornament.

Varying the lengths of the grid will give this trellis a bit of an Asian influence in its design. This project can be done with copper or brass wire over the bamboo joints or simply hand-tied in raffia, if you prefer (however, the raffia will not be as long-lasting).

1. Lay out bamboo poles in a design of your liking. For our project we created a series of 1'×1' square grids and then varied the length of some of the interior poles. Poles can be cut to length with either a miter saw or a handsaw. It is important to note that top, bottom, and two side poles should connect to one another and extend the entire perimeter of the trellis to create a stable frame on which to attach all the other variously sized poles.

2. Once the two vertical end poles have been identified, use the ¾" paddle bit to bore out the center of the pole bottom. This will allow for poles to slip easily over rebar that will be set in the ground to act as an anchor for holding the trellis upright.

3. Reposition top, bottom, and two side perimeter poles and attach together. The poles should be attached by first predrilling holes for screws. Be sure not to drill completely through both poles, only the back pole and the back side of face pole. Attach ⅝" wood screw from back side and, using aviation safety wire pliers, wrap brass or copper wire or raffia around two poles. The twisted side of wire should also be on back side of trellis.

4. Once the four perimeter poles have been secured to one another, add all the additional interior poles, attaching them to one another with the same process.

5. To erect trellis, find a suitable location and mark the spot where the two end poles sit. Using a hammer or mallet, pound rebar into the ground at these points. Leave about 8" to 12" of rebar extended out aboveground and slip bamboo poles of trellis over rebar.

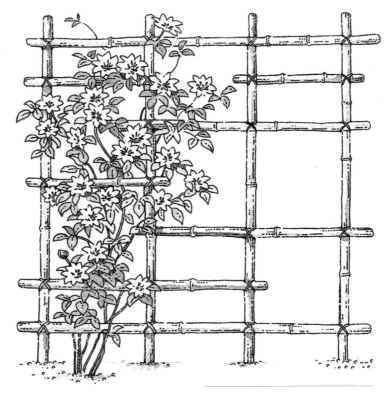

The square grid design of this trellis can be varied to suit your taste

MATERIALS AND TOOLS

Scissors

Plant cuttings

Newspaper

Flower press (see Notes)

Cardboard

Household white glue

Spray bottle

11½"×16½" sheets of
herbarium paper, 100
percent rag paper, or
nonacidic archival paper
(available at most art
supply stores)

Wax paper

Paper towels

Blotting paper

Calligraphy pen or pencil

Flat weight such as a heavy
board or book

 Herbarium specimens have long been made by botanists, reaching a peak with adventurer-naturalists Joseph Banks, who sailed with Captain Cook, and Alfred Russel Wallace. These pressed and mounted dried plant specimens are now coveted by antique dealers and collectors as art for framing. What started out as a representation of the living plant for scientific study has evolved into something of an art form.

Although you may not be chronicling the findings from your latest expedition into the wilds of Asia, Africa, or Australia, preserving plants from your own garden can help brighten a bedroom wall—and your spirits in the off season.

Though most specimens are collected when the plant is in flower or fruit for scientific reasons, the aesthetic motivation for doing so will be obvious as well.

1. Take clippings of plants that you wish to preserve. Ideally, take cuttings that include flowers, fruits, or the plant in seed.

2. Lay out first specimen on top of a piece of newspaper on top of bottom board of flower press. Limp plants work well because you can fold back leaves and flowers to show off all the plant's features to best advantage. Once set in place and arranged, place a piece of newspaper over the specimen.

3. Place a piece of cardboard on top of the newspaper and repeat process with another specimen. Continue as desired, then close the flower press and cinch ties as tightly as possible. Set press in a warm, dry place (for instance, an attic in the summer) and allow specimens to dry for one week.

4. Dilute white household glue (approximately 3 parts glue to 4 parts water) and put into a spray bottle.

5. Set a piece of herbarium paper on a flat work surface (a board works well, since it can easily be moved during drying process if necessary). Remove first specimen from flower press. Arrange specimen on paper so that you are happy with the layout of the page.

6. Lift specimen and spray the back side of it with the diluted glue. Carefully set specimen on herbarium paper and blot any glue that leaks out from behind the specimen with paper towel.

7. Write the name of the plant on the paper, as well as the date and location of where the specimen was collected.

8. Cover paper and specimen with wax paper.

9. Place blotting paper and a weight on the specimen and allow the herbarium specimen to dry for a few days. Frame as desired.

Flower presses are available at most craft stores. You can set up a homemade version with two 12"×18" pieces of plywood, putting several layers of cardboard between them and, when you are ready to use the press, cinching it shut with 2 straps.

If you wish, the specimen can then be framed and hung, although it is best to hang framed picture out of direct sun. Of course, the specimens used by arboretums and botanical gardens are stored in a cool, dark, dry place for safekeeping.

MATERIALS AND TOOLS

Scissors

Disposable gloves (several pairs)

Cuttings of poison ivy or other toxic plants

An old phone book

Disposable tablecloth or craft paper, to protect your work surface

Household white glue

Spray bottle (optional)

Calligraphy pen (optional)

Sheets of 100 percent rag paper

Glass frame with side clips

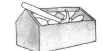 The ability to identify plants isn't always merely a luxury. In the case of plants like poison ivy and poison oak, and of phototoxic garden plants such as castor beans and euphorbias, being able to spot them can prevent you from getting contact dermatitis. Placing a simple herbarium specimen of such plants in a frame under glass allows children and houseguests to learn which plants to avoid without exposing them to the oils that cause people to react to these plants.

Poison ivy grows throughout most of the United States and Canada. It grows as ground cover, shrub, or vine, climbing high into trees, so it can be hard to identify. Its leaves are often confused with those of raspberries and other berries (although berries' stems have spines on them). The three leaflets of poison ivy can also have leaves that vary from smooth margined to notched, depending on the plant. Its fall color is an unmistakable brilliant red. Although a few over-the-counter medications can counteract the oils in poison ivy and these other plants, a little bit of knowledge and an ability to identify the plants before coming into contact with them is undoubtedly the best "cure" of all.

It bears repeating: while making this project, be careful, while working with these specimens, to avoid coming in contact with their oils.

1. Wear long sleeves, long pants, and disposable gloves to take cuttings. Take cuttings that clearly show the three-leaf construction of the plant. Include full-grown and young leaves, as they vary in form.

2. Use an old phone book that can be thrown away after use to press the plants. Set specimens between pages and set in a cool, dry place. Specimens should be dry in about 1 week. When they are sufficiently dry, prepare to put them in your frame.

3. Before working with specimens, again put on clean long pants, long sleeves, and disposable gloves, and cover work surface with disposable tablecloth or craft paper. Cut paper to fit frame, if necessary. Select cuttings and lay out on paper. Arrange them on the page, and, if desired, remove leaves. Use calligraphy pen, if desired, to label with plant name and identifying characteristics such as "Poison Ivy" and the standard phrase "leaves of three, let it be," below where the leaves will be set. Reset specimens and put a tiny dab of glue behind the leaves to hold them in place. If preferred, the glue can be mixed, 1 part to 10, with water in a spray bottle and sprayed on back of plant.

4. Place the glass over the specimen and the clips on the sides to hold the glass in place.

5. Take great care in cleaning up work area. Wearing fresh disposable gloves, throw away the table covering. Wash any cutting tools with soap and water. Carefully remove gloves and dispose of them. Wash your hands with cool, soapy water. Wear a fresh pair of gloves to clean the glass and frame and remove any fingerprints that may retain toxic oils. Dispose of gloves.

6. Hang the pressed poison ivy in a location where it can be easily seen.

TILLANDSIA MOBILE

MATERIALS

2 metal lampshade rings
(washer tops), one 10" in
diameter and one 14" in
diameter, available through
lamp supply shops
Thin copper or brass craft
wire
Tillandsias, or air plants, in a
variety of forms and colors

TOOLS

Wire cutters
Measuring tape
Shepherd's hook (optional)

 Epiphytes are plants that do not grow in soil but fulfill their nutritional needs by taking nutrients from the air and from debris collected in the crooks of trees that they inhabit. Many orchids are epiphytic, and so is another wonderful range of epiphytes, the *Tillandsia* genus, or, as they are commonly known, air plants.

Tillandsia is a genus of bromeliads from the Americas, mostly in subtropical, semiarid areas. There are hundreds of species, from silver-foliaged species that are more sun and drought tolerant to soft green foliaged species that have spidery, spiky leaves like creatures from outer space. Tillandsias prefer bright filtered light (strong direct sunlight will dry them out). They make long-lived houseplants and, depending on their environment, require water once a week at most and often only once a month. Tillandsias tend to dry out indoors, so it is a good idea to water them by entirely immersing the plants in the sink overnight on a monthly basis. Tillandsias are frost sensitive, so move these mobiles indoors in colder weather.

This mobile was inspired by a Calderesque mobile made in the 1970s by British designer David Hicks. Here, by using simple lampshade forms known as washer tops instead of attaching each plant on its own cantilever, the project becomes a much less complicated balancing act. This mobile looks great hanging from the ceiling in the center of a room, in a doorway, over a table set for a special event, or in its natural home—a child's bedroom.

1. Measure and cut three 22" pieces of wire. Neatly twist each piece around the 14"-diameter washer top, positioning them where the three spokes are attached to the ring. Pull 3 wires together over center of washer top and hold above work surface to pull them together in the middle. Hold the ring off the work surface to check its balance and, when balanced, twist all 3 wires together, leaving about 2 inches of wire above twist to fashion into a loop from which to hang washer top.

2. Fashion loop out of remaining wire by twisting it back against initial point where 3 wires converge. Hang the washer top by loop on shepherd's hook or other hook to suspend it above work surface.

3. Take second washer top and attach it to the top washer top with wire. First attach three 18 to 24" lengths of wire to lower washer top near spokes and then bring lengths up to spokes of upper washer top and attach the two together, making sure to keep the second washer top parallel with top one, at desired distance from upper washer top.

4. Starting with the upper washer top, select air plants to hang from it and attach them, first by wrapping one end of a 14" length of wire around middle of plant, weaving wire amid plant's leaves, and then wrapping opposite end of wire around washer top at desired height. Repeat with other plants, trying to create a sense of balance when hanging plants and using a range of colors, textures, and sizes for visual interest. Vary the lengths of wire so that the plants are spaced irregularly.

5. Continue adding air plants to mobile until desired effect is achieved. Adjust small and large plants and slide plants along wire to keep mobile in balance. Water plants thoroughly. Place mobile in a spot near a window with bright, filtered light.

FRUIT

Given that a plant produces fruit in order to attract animals to eat and disperse its seeds, it is no wonder that we love these delectable botanical forms. And while their natural sugars and contrasting acids are developed to peak after the seeds mature, the fruit also reaches its most beautiful form when fully ripened.

FETA CHEESE AND WATERMELON SALAD
WITH RASPBERRY VINAIGRETTE

SERVES 4 TO 6

1 small seedless watermelon

2 pints fresh raspberries, rinsed clean and picked over

1 cup light olive oil

$\frac{1}{3}$ cup good-quality raspberry vinegar

6 cups spinach or watercress, cleaned and dried

12 ounces feta cheese, crumbled

Salt and freshly ground pepper, to taste

This salad was first developed by Jacquie Borden, who catered the meals for *Cultivating Life*. It became such a lunchtime favorite of the crew that we knew we had to have Jacquie on the show to make it. Her straightforward fresh food epitomizes the best of outdoor dining: local ingredients used creatively at the peak of its season. On the set, we would leave the dressing on the side so that the salad didn't get soggy and was always freshly dressed. Leftover vinaigrette may be stored in an airtight container in the refrigerator for up to one week. • *Photograph on page 118*

1. Using the small side of a melon baller, scoop out about 25 balls from watermelon and set aside. Reserve several tablespoons of watermelon juice.

2. For the vinaigrette, place 1 pint of raspberries, olive oil, and vinegar in a blender and puree until smooth. Add several tablespoons of reserved watermelon juice to the vinaigrette, if you like. Strain the mixture through a fine-mesh sieve and discard the seeds; set vinaigrette aside.

3. Arrange spinach or watercress on serving platter, and garnish with melon balls, remaining raspberries, and feta cheese. Pour desired amount of vinaigrette over salad, season with salt and pepper, and serve.

SMALL-BATCH PRESERVES

MAKES ABOUT 1 CUP

1 cup ripe or overripe fruit, roughly chopped

3 tablespoons dark brown sugar

1 teaspoon finely grated citrus zest from a lime, orange, or lemon

2 teaspoons citrus juice

Chopped crystallized ginger or other flavoring such as cinnamon and herbs (optional)

Putting up jars of homemade jams is an American tradition, but you can also make a small batch in a saucepan and keep it in the fridge for short-term use without having to sterilize dozens of jars. These easy-to-make jams, perfect for topping toast or setting between layers of cake, are an ideal way to use up overripe fruit such as apricots, plums, blueberries, peaches, or even leftover rhubarb. You can also combine several fruits or add some chopped crystallized ginger or grated nutmeg. Strawberry-ginger jam is a perfect dessert simply spooned over a dish of plain yogurt.

1. In a medium saucepan, combine all the ingredients and bring to a boil over medium heat.

2. Reduce heat and simmer for 20 to 30 minutes, until thickened. Remove from heat and allow to cool to room temperature. Store in a jar, refrigerated, up to 2 weeks.

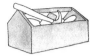 This project is based on old-fashioned orangery planters that were used to set out citrus trees in the garden; they also held a multitude of other plants on a terrace or along an old walkway in the garden. They were raised off the ground to provide the orange and lemon trees with good air circulation, which helped prevent disease, but the legs also give the planter an elegant look.

The tapered design of these planters requires a little attention to detail, so follow the directions closely.

MATERIALS

One 2"×4"×12' red cedar board

One 1"×8"×10' red cedar board

One 1"×8"×8' red cedar board

1½" and 2½" stainless steel screws

Exterior wood glue

TOOLS

Pencil

Tape measure

Carpenter's square

Hammer

Coping saw

Plug cutter

Drill

Screw bit, screw gun, or screwdriver

Countersink drill bit

Table saw

Dado blade set

Miter saw

Palm sander

Fine-grade sandpaper

Wood finish

1. Using table saw, rip down 2"×4"×12' cedar board into two 18", two 21", and two 22" lengths, and then rip each of these lengths down into 1½"×1½" (nominal) lengths. You will end up with four 1½"×1½"×18" pieces, four 1½"×1½"×21" pieces, and four 1½"×1½"×22" pieces.

2. Using a miter saw, create planter legs by cutting 10-degree angles at *both* ends of 21" lengths, bringing each piece down to a finished length of 20". These angles must be cut with board being held at a 45-degree angle to where the board will normally lay flat (so that the 10-degree angle runs from one corner of board to the opposite corner). It is best to create a jig to keep the corner stable while making these cuts. Trim top and bottom ends of leg with 10-degree angles so that angles are parallel to one another (angled in the same direction).

3. Using miter saw, cut 7-degree angles at ends of 18" pieces for a finished length of 17" on short side of the board. Unlike the angles on the planter legs, these brackets will have end angles that face away from each other. Using table saw, set blade to a 7-degree angle and rip a 7-degree bevel down the length of 17" legs, making sure the bevel is applied to long side of board where angles create the greatest distance.

4. Install a ⅜" dado blade on table saw set to a depth of ½". The fence should be set ⅜" away from the near side of the blade. Set the four 20" legs in place and identify the inside corner of each leg. The 2 sides adjacent to this corner are where grooves will be cut out. Place a mark on each 20" leg, 3¼" from bottom. Use the dado blade to create a groove from top of each leg down to this mark.

5. Test-fit bottom brackets to 4 legs. The bottom bracket should be attached 3" from bottom of each leg, with 7-degree beveled side facing up. The brackets should be fastened to legs by screwing 2½" screws through corner of each leg to abutting bracket. Be sure to set screws so those attaching each bracket do not hit one another. Predrill holes and countersink screws; apply glue to each joint.

[CONTINUED]

6. With planter frame completed, make side panels for planter. Using stock 1"×8" boards with an actual dimension of ⅝"×7¼", cut out four 22" lengths from 10' length and four 20" lengths from each 8' length. On each of 20" lengths, mark out and cut a 7-degree angle on width of the board. Repeat at opposite end of board so that long-side dimension is 19½" and short-side dimension is 17¾". On each of the 22" lengths, mark out and cut a 7-degree angle on width of the board. Repeat at opposite end of board so that long-side dimension is 21¼" and short-side dimension is 19½".

7. Install a ½" dado blade on table saw and set to a height of ⁵⁄₁₆". Adjust the fence to allow for just the end ½" of each panel to run over the dado blade, then notch out angled ends of panels on face side. Dry-fit each panel into notches on planter frame and trim ends if necessary.

8. Measure length of each side of planter just above panels and cut remaining 1½"×1½"×22" to length with same 7-degree angle at each end. Also rip down length of each top piece at a 7-degree angle to sit flush with top of legs. Before attaching each of these pieces the same way the bottom brackets are attached (step 5), be sure to remove the side panels, add glue to the notched areas, and reinsert. The void left by the notches at the top of each leg can be filled by cutting small square plugs and gluing into place.

9. Cut out eight 1½"×18½" slats from remaining 1×8 stock and space them evenly apart inside bottom of the planter with each end resting on inside of bottom bracket. Fasten each end with 1½" screws.

10. Finally, cut out plugs from scrap and plug remaining screw holes, trim flush with coping saw, sand lightly, and add your finish of choice.

Growing citrus isn't as complicated as many gardeners think, even for those who live in areas where citrus can't stay outside year-round. With some good advice from our friend Byron Martin, of Logee's Tropical Plants in Danielson, Connecticut, and the right care, you can grow lemons, limes, kumquats, and oranges.

All citrus need plenty of light to develop and maintain a healthy root system. The root systems of citrus grown in containers require a period of dry-down to help prevent root disease. Avoid potting into a container that is too large. Even when planting up a rootbound plant, do not increase the pot size by more than an inch or two in diameter. Also, planting in terra-cotta pots helps plants to dry down properly between watering. It's best to water only when the surface of the soil is visibly dry.

The best growing temperature is from slightly above freezing up to 80 or 90 degrees F., with the exception of Key lime, which needs temperatures above 60 degrees F. Before setting citrus out for the summer, adjust the plant slowly to full sun and any change in temperature—otherwise the leaves will scald from the sun or go into shock from too quick a temperature change.

Citrus have problems with micronutrient deficiencies, so be sure to use a balanced fertilizer. Fertilizer can help induce flowers, but too much can promote leafy growth over flowers. Therefore, fertilize plants only during active growth, never in dormant periods. And when you get lemons, make lemonade.

GRAINS AND SEEDS

The final stage in a plant's reproductive cycle, seeds and grains are the staff of life. From wheat or rice used to feed humans or animals to heirloom tomato seeds that create more of their own fruit, nutrient-rich seeds contain a world within their confines and have been collected for centuries so that the world can continue to sustain itself—and preserve the plants we love. Their germination is a thing of beauty, whether the young seedling is being grown for the garden or simply sprouted for a salad.

MATERIALS

Three 1"×12"×12' rough-cut
    pine boards
One 2"×4"×8' pine board
Eight 3" exterior-grade
    galvanized corner braces
1¼" and 2½" exterior-grade
    wood screws
Soil

TOOLS

Tape measure
Circular saw
Framing square
Drill with screw bit
Pencil
5-pound mallet

 Raised beds have been used for ages in areas where soil is poor or doesn't drain well, but they also have other purposes. The soil warms more quickly in a raised bed, allowing us to start vegetables earlier in the garden. They are also great for growing seedlings of young perennials that would be overwhelmed by mature plants if set out in the garden before they develop.

These seedbeds can be designed to any size, although it is best to keep them narrow enough for you to tend without stepping into the bed itself. Pine will weather to gray over time, but if you like, an investment in red cedar will extend the life of your raised bed. • *Photograph on page 126*

1. With circular saw, trim ends of each 1×12 board so they accurately measure 12'. Cut one of the 12' boards into two 6' lengths. Cut 2×4 into eight 1' wooden stakes.

2. Position four 1×12 boards into a rectangle set on edge and attach each corner with two of the corner braces. At each corner, attach 1 brace 3" from top and the other 3" from bottom using 1¼" screws. Use a framing square to be sure the box is square. Alternatively, you can measure corner to diagonal corner and adjust the box until both measurements are equal.

3. Set box in place and adjust if it is still not square. Pound the stakes into ground to a depth of 6 inches at inside of each of 4 corners of box as well as 4' from the end of each of the 12' boards. Fasten box to stakes using screws.

4. Fill with soil and plant.

storing seeds

Seed savers and sproutheads alike know there is much that can be done to keep seeds viable. Even so, not many could imagine sprouting a 2,000-year-old seed, like that of a rare woody plant that was germinated several years ago in Israel.

Most seeds, if properly stored, will be viable for 1 to 8 years. Here are some simple tips:

• Store in a cool, dry place (55 to 70 degrees F. and with a humidity of 70 percent or less). Every decrease of 10 degrees F. in storage temperature doubles the seed storage life at temperatures above freezing. Every 1 percent decrease in seed moisture content doubles seed storage life.

• Add packets of silica gel to container to keep humidity low.

• Store out of direct light.

• Storing in a sealed jar can double shelf life.

Making a cork-lined frame to highlight seed packets, botanical specimens, or a pretty dried seed head is one way of keeping your gardening inspirations at hand.

1. Remove backing of frame and measure opening. If frame opening is larger than one cork square, you will have to connect squares. To do this, run a thin line of glue along one side of cork square and butt another square up to glue line. Hold it in place until dry.

2. With the mat knife and straightedge, cut cork to size of frame opening.

3. Reattach frame backing.

4. On back side of cork, run a thin line of glue around outer edges and continue in a spiral until back of board is covered lightly with glue.

5. Place cork, glue side down, onto frame backing. It should fit snugly within frame opening. Allow glue to dry.

6. With insect pins, pushpins, or thumbtacks, attach dried flowers, seed packets, or whatever inspires you to cork.

MATERIALS AND TOOLS

1 frame with an interior space of less than 12"×12" (glass removed)
Measuring tape
Quick-drying craft glue, such as Fabri-Tac
One 12"×12" cork square
Mat knife
Straightedge
Seed packets, dried seed heads, ferns, etc.
Cutting board
Insect pins (available from science supply stores), pushpins, or thumbtacks

NOTE

Thicker cork in the ¼" to ¾" range is best so tacks have something to stick into.

mustard from seed

Some foods have become so ingrained in our lives in their prepared forms that we don't even think about where they come from. For instance, when we decided to do an episode of *Cultivating Life* on seeds, we thought about all the seeds we use in cooking (e.g., sesame seeds, poppy seeds, mustard seeds) and then realized that we had never even thought of mustard as a seed by-product—let alone as something we could make ourselves. With a little experimentation, we discovered that making mustard is relatively easy, and that a jar of homemade mustard has a taste all its own.

Try different herbs and wine to come up with flavor combinations you love. Homemade mustard is a perfect signature gift.

For either of the recipes below, you'll need 2 sterilized glass jars and lids.

1. In a small bowl, combine dry ingredients. Slowly add cold beer and stir. Transfer to a saucepan.

2. Heat mixture on stove over medium-high heat until it reaches a near-boil. Simmer to thicken. Pour into sterilized glass jars. Store in the refrigerator; allow 1 week for flavor to deepen.

MAKES 1 CUP

¾ cup dry mustard powder (hot or mild)

½ cup brown sugar

1 teaspoon salt

¼ cup mixed mustard seeds, crushed

⅔ cup cold, dark beer

GRAINY WHITE WINE AND HONEY HERB MUSTARD

1. In a small saucepan, combine wine, onion, garlic, and herbs and bring to a boil. Lower heat and simmer for 5 minutes. Cool to room temperature, then strain through a fine sieve. Reserve clear liquid.

2. In another small saucepan, combine cooled seasoned liquid with dry mustard powder, mustard seeds, honey, oil, and salt. Heat slowly, stirring constantly until the mixture thickens. Pour into sterilized glass jars and refrigerate. Allow several days for flavor to deepen.

MAKES 1½ CUPS

2 cups dry white wine

1 cup chopped onion

2 crushed garlic cloves

Mixed fresh herbs such as rosemary, sage, and tarragon

4 tablespoons dry mustard powder (mild)

½ cup brown mustard seeds

½ cup yellow mustard seeds

2 tablespoons mild honey

1 tablespoon vegetable oil

2 teaspoons salt

RIGHT Growing Microgreens (page 134)

LEFT Growing Sprouts (page 135)

MATERIALS

Seeds

Sprouting container (for seeds
that need presprouting
before planting)

Sterilized seed-starting mix or
potting soil

Clean plastic container with
bottom drainage (added
by poking holes through
bottom)

Terra-cotta pot

Organic water-soluble
fertilizer (optional)

TOOLS

Spray bottle

Clear plastic bag

Microgreens have become increasingly popular for their delicate flavors and wonderful taste. These greens are the next step forward from sprouting—and continuing to grow them for their colorful leaves, which can then be harvested and eaten. From red cabbage and arugula to cress and mustard and radish greens, these baby greens are filled with nutrition and can be harvested as they leaf out—and for those with limited space, they can even be cultivated on a windowsill, provided there is good air circulation.

Different seeds have different needs. For the best results, read up on each type of seed before beginning. Most greens will be ready to harvest in 4 to 14 days. Some seeds need to be soaked overnight or sprouted before planting. However, mucilaginous seeds such as arugula are never soaked; instead, they're sown directly on top of moist soil. Gelatin sacs form around each seed to help hold in moisture during germination.

Growing greens with kids is a great way of involving them in gardening and maybe even increasing the appeal of salads and greens. A simple seed-starting tray and lid work well, but an attractive cachepot allows you to leave them front and center as they develop. Red amaranth greens (which have a nutty taste that's great in salads) are so beautiful that they have the appeal of a great houseplant while they are growing. • *Photograph on page 133*

1. Prepare seeds by soaking in sprouter, if necessary, following directions on seed package. Some seeds, such as arugula, do not require sprouting. Fill a clean container or pot with moist seed-starting mix or potting soil.

2. Add 1 to 2 inches of soil to selected container. Spread seeds evenly on top of soil. Gently mist the seeds with a spray bottle of water. The seeds should be moistened but not swimming. Place container or pot near a window but out of direct sunlight. If using a plastic container, cover it to hold in moisture until the seeds germinate; if using a terra-cotta pot, cover it with a plastic bag during germination. Once tiny roots form, open lid or remove plastic bag and place container in a location with good air circulation and indirect light for the balance of growing period.

3. Keep the soil evenly moist, but not soggy, by misting seedlings with a spray bottle. As the roots grow in, water more deeply and less frequently, never allowing water to pool around young seedlings.

4. Depending on the greens, harvest in 4 to 14 days. If cut back with scissors, some greens will put on a second flush of growth like cut-and-come-again lettuce and can be harvested again when new growth has developed.

When starting seeds, gardeners marvel at the miracle of germinating seeds, but they may not think of growing these delicate sprouts for eating. With the use of a simple plastic sprouter or a hemp bag, they are easy to grow, amazingly fresh and tasty, and nutritious to boot.

Sprouts are full of protein, vitamins, minerals, and antioxidants, as well as enzymes that aid in digestion. They also just taste good. Bean and alfalfa sprouts are familiar to many North Americans, but broccoli, radish, fennel, and onion sprouts are equally delicious and add a subtle version of their adult flavor to salads. Sprouted almonds and peanuts make a perfect snack on their own.

As in the garden, a small amount of seeds may make five to ten times as much plant materials, so keep this in mind when starting sprouts. • *Photograph on page 132*

1. Cull seeds, nuts, or beans to remove any debris.

2. Rinse seeds, nuts, or beans to remove any particles of dust or dirt.

3. Soak seeds, nuts, or beans in 2 to 3 times as much water (i.e., 1 cup of water to ½ or ⅓ cup seeds). Stir to ensure that all of the seeds make contact with the water. Soaking times vary depending on choice of seed, so it is important to read package directions. As a general rule, 8 to 12 hours is the right amount of time (although some need to soak for only 20 minutes and others do not require soaking at all—again, read instructions). The seed coat should start to swell when seeds are ready to be drained.

4. Rinse and drain seeds, nuts, or beans in cool water (60 to 70 degrees F.) every 6 to 12 hours for the next 2 to 6 days, depending on what is being sprouted. Place in a spot with good air circulation to ensure healthy sprout growth. Seeds, nuts, and beans do not need light to sprout, but once they develop tiny leaves they need to be in indirect light for 1 or 2 days so they can green up. (Plants do not perform photosynthesis until leaves develop.) As a general rule, nuts are ready to eat in 12 to 24 hours, beans take about 2 to 3 days, and other seeds 1 to 14 days.

5. Sprouts will store well in the refrigerator if they are dry. Let them dry for about 12 hours after last rinsing before putting in refrigerator. Drying process may be sped up by putting sprouts in a salad spinner. Store them in dry plastic sprouter or in a plastic bag. You can buy special bags for storage that will keep vegetables fresh for up to a month.

6. Sterilize your sprouter every 3 or 4 crops by soaking it in a solution of bleach and water for 10 to 20 minutes (1 tablespoon of bleach per pint of water), then scrub it thoroughly with soap and water.

MATERIALS

Dry beans, nuts, grains, sproutable seeds, available through health food stores or The Sprout People (see Resources)

Water

TOOL

Sprouter (hemp bag or easy sprouter)

some seeds to consider

LEAFY SPROUTS: alfalfa, clover, and gourmet mixes, which may include arugula, cress, radish, fenugreek, mizuna, tatsoi, and others

BEANS: mung, garbanzos, peanut, lentils, peas, adzuki

BRASSICA FAMILY: broccoli, radish, arugula, mustard, cress

GRAINS: wheat, spelt, quinoa, buckwheat, rye, kamut

NUTS: almonds

MATERIALS

6 pots of rice plants such as 'Red Dragon'

A long container for planting that will hold water, such as a pig trough or an oblong galvanized pot

Potting mix

Stones or other decorative mulch such as marbles or glass mulch

Water

Rice is the most widely consumed grain in the world and is grown in Italy, Asia, Louisiana, and elsewhere. Its ornamental qualities are often overlooked, a fact that is mysterious for anyone who has ever seen a rice field in cultivation. From its chartreuse spring growth to its fall seed heads, this plant has a wonderful romantic quality.

Rice can be grown in standing water. Because the water-soaked soil in the container will not dry out quickly, rice makes an ideal potted planting for those who don't have time to constantly water their containers. If rice plants are unavailable at a local nursery, they can easily be started by seed in pots and planted after they develop.

Rice looks best in a series of clumps (as it is planted in the field), and top-dressing the soil with colorful stones or glass mulch or marbles will give the final result an even more romantic look. A cultivar such as the carmine-leaved *Oryza sativa* 'Red Dragon' makes a stunning planting in a long, narrow container (such as this pig trough) that will hold water.

1. Space plants evenly across length of container. Because the water-filled container will be quite heavy when planted, select a sunny location where container can remain and plant in place. Fill in around plants with potting mix.

2. Place a layer of decorative mulch around the clumps of rice up to top of container and add water to fill trough. If perlite from the potting mix floats to the top, add more water until water in container is clear, allowing perlite to run out over top of container.

3. Keep container well watered for a season. The rice will develop toward end of season and can be collected to be grown again the next year.

MATERIALS AND TOOLS

Fiber, such as kozo, iris leaves, or other fibrous plants

Scissors

Saucepan large enough to hold fibers and water to cover

Blender

Rectangular plastic tub large enough to accommodate mold and deckle

Flower petals, seeds, grass clippings (optional)

Mold and deckle (available online or at art supply stores)

Felt mat large enough to accommodate mold and deckle

Rice paper *(washi)* is not really made from rice. The paper referred to by this name is usually made from kozo fiber, from the bark of a Japanese mulberry plant. Papermaker Suzi Cozzens told us, however, that you can also use plants from your own backyard to create this thin, translucent yet remarkably strong paper. In fact, any fibrous cellulose material can become the foundation material.

If you wish to collect your own fiber for making this paper, try using the leaves of an iris or another fibrous plant. You may also want to collect flower petals, small seeds, grass, and other colorful natural materials to add as decoration (this material will provide interest but not structure to the paper). To create the very thinnest paper, buy kozo fiber to add to the materials collected from the garden.

Though there is an art to making rice paper, experimentation is the best way to refine your craft.

1. Soak kozo or other dried fiber until it softens up somewhat. (If using fresh materials from the garden, skip this step.)

2. Cut fibers into a manageable length and then cook them until they become tender. Drain the fiber. Process fiber in the blender. You can try processing the fiber lightly or heavily and see how the resulting paper differs. Both will work.

3. Fill the tub with cold water and add blended fiber. The amount of fiber you add will determine thickness of paper. Try adding a small portion first and see how your first sheet comes out by testing steps 4 and 5. Continue adding more fiber to water as you see fit or until you reach desired thickness of paper. Add flower petals, seeds, or grasses to mixture, if desired.

4. Stir water to suspend fiber, then in one gentle, smooth motion plunge mold and deckle into water and fiber mixture and pull it up out of the water. Rock gently to even out fiber on its surface.

5. Remove deckle, the picture-frame portion of the mold and deckle. Flip the mold over and release wet paper onto felt mat by gently rocking mold back and forth until paper is released. Set aside to dry. Peel off felt when dry.

Delicate *washi,* commonly referred to as rice paper, can be applied, using a waterproof sealer, to the surface of clear glass objects such as cylindrical vases, simple plates, and votives. The paper's translucent quality comes to the fore in the same way as in a shoji screen or a rice paper lantern.

Of course, if you are creating votives the glass should be flameproof. If you are creating dishes, make sure your sealer is nontoxic and bear in mind that the pieces should be washed by hand in warm water.

MATERIALS

Paintbrush

Clear nontoxic waterproof
   sealer

Clear plate, cylindrical vase,
   or votive

1 sheet *washi* (rice paper),
   lace paper, or watermark
   paper

Scissors or mat knife

1. Cut a piece of rice paper slightly larger than dish, vase, or votive to be covered. For a cylindrical vase or votive, simply roll vase over paper one complete turn to get a sense of diameter.

2. Using paintbrush, apply clear waterproof sealer evenly on back of clear glass plate or exterior of vase or votive. Set rice paper carefully in place, trying to minimize any folds or creases in paper. Using more sealer, brush rice paper down so that it lies flat against the surface.

3. Apply another clear coat of sealer to rice paper to saturate paper thoroughly and seal it to glass. Carefully trim edges with scissors or mat knife.

4. Set aside to dry. Add another coat of sealer, if necessary.

FAUNA

We have always enjoyed chronicling the world around us. Studying nature and connecting ourselves to creatures great and small comes instinctively to humans, whether we are attracting birds and butterflies to our backyards with plants and bird feeders or making things for our homes inspired by natural forms.

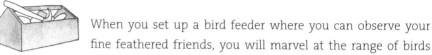

MATERIALS

One 1"×8"×5' cedar board

1' of ³⁄₈" wood doweling

Exterior wood glue

#7 stainless steel screws, 1⅝" long

8 stainless steel screws, 1½" long

One 4"×16" pane of glass, ⅛" thick

2' of ³⁄₁₆" synthetic rope

Two #14 brass screw eyes

One 1½" brass screw hook

One 1½" brass hinge

Shepherd's hook (optional)

TOOLS

Pencil

Tape measure

Table saw with a ⅛" blade

Miter saw

Drill press

Drill

Screw bit, screw gun, or screwdriver

⁷⁄₃₂" wood bit

Countersink drill bit

1" paddle bit

³⁄₈" wood bit

2 Quick-Grip 36" clamps

Ruler

Black permanent marker

Glass cutter

Pencil

When you set up a bird feeder where you can observe your fine feathered friends, you will marvel at the range of birds that pass through your backyard. Making this beautiful feeder yourself means that even when birds aren't out there feeding, there is something handsome to look at. The glass panels let you see in a glance from the kitchen window when the feeder needs to be restocked. · *Photograph on page 140*

1. Begin by assembling roof and bottom door. Cut two 7" lengths from 1×8 cedar board and rip each down to 1"×5"×7". Reserve scrap cedar. Stack ripped-down boards on top of one another, glue, and clamp together. Once dry, cut block to 4½"×6". Mark 2 points on either end of short sides ³⁄₈" in from the edge and 2¼" in from long sides. Drill a ⁷⁄₃₂" hole at these two points. These will be used for hanging the feeder with a rope. Laying block flat, mark 1⅛" in on all 4 sides and set the miter saw to a 45-degree angle. Cut angles outward from these marks to create a chamfer.

2. Using miter or table saw, cut out a 1"×2"×3⁷⁄₁₆" piece from reserved leftover cedar for bottom door. At a 45-degree angle, use table saw to trim off material on one of 3½" sides so door will be able to swing open freely when attached later.

3. Next, cut out 2 sides with feeder holes. Cut an 18" length from remaining 1×8 stock and rip down into two 1"×3½"×18" pieces. Use a pencil to scribe a center line the length of each of 1"×3½"×18" pieces. Next, place marks on that center line at 1½", 3½", 7", 9", 12½", and 14½" from bottom. Using drill press and 1" paddle bit, bore holes through the 3½", 9", and 14½" marks. Bore holes using the ³⁄₈" bit ½ inch into the 1½", 7", and 12½" marks. Not drilling completely through these holes will create a stop for the dowel perches.

4. Next, fabricate the 2 sides with the glass windows. Cut a 22" length from 1×8 stock and rip down to four ¾"×1"×22" and one ¾"×1"×10". Using a standard table saw blade with a width of ⅛", dado out one side of each of the four 22" pieces. The dado should be centered in the ¾" side of the cedar piece and set at a depth of ¼". Repeat this dado cut on both ¾" sides of the 10" piece.

5. Out of the four 22" lengths, create 2 frames that are 3½"×18". Using miter saw, cut corners of the frame at 45 degrees. Also cut out four 1½" lengths from the 10" piece. These will be used as spacers for windowpanes.

6. Cut pane of glass into six 1⅞"×5⅛" pieces with glass cutter. (You should also be able to get these cut at your local hardware store.)

7. Dry-fit frame with panes of glass and spacers. Once fitted properly, attach glass, spacers, and frames with wood glue. Fasten with 1⅝" narrow-head stainless steel screws from short ends of frame, being sure to predrill screw holes to prevent splitting of wood. Clamp each frame at center spacers, as these are held together only with glue.

8. Next, create canopies or baffles that prevent the seed from spilling out of the seed-dispensing holes. Rip down the 2"×4"×12" into a 1½"×1½"×12" piece. Using the table saw, cut out a 1¼"×1¼" block from length of piece. You will be left with ¼" L-shaped piece that will act as hood over the 6 seed holes. Set aside.

9. Attach 2 window sides to one of the seed-hole sides using wood glue and 1½" screws, being sure to countersink screws for plugging later. The seed-hole side should sit flush on the inside of the window side so that the screws are attached from the window side.

10. Dry-fit remaining seed-hole side. Measure the space between 2 seed-hole sides and cut out 3 baffles or hoods from V-shaped pieces to this length. Using wood glue, attach the 3 baffles directly over each seed hole to create a canopy. Refit and attach remaining seed-hole side to baffles and other 3 sides with glue and screws.

11. Complete final assembly. Add 2 screw eyes ½" from the top and on center of each window side. Attach brass hinge to both the bottom door and base of bird feeder. Drill a pilot hole in window side opposite hinge. Be sure hole is centered to go through the side and into bottom door. Insert screw hook to secure door in a closed position. Snake rope through the 2 holes of the roof and tie knots on the bottom side of screw eyes.

12. Cut six 2" dowels, glue ends, and insert in holes beneath seed holes to create perches. Plug countersink holes and sand flush, if you like.

13. Fill and hang bird feeder. (Since cedar is a soft wood, you may wish to hang the feeder on a shepherd's hook with a baffle so that squirrels will have a hard time getting at it.)

MATERIALS

One 1"×12"×4' red cedar
  board

#7 stainless steel screws, 1⅝"
  long

Copper flashing

¾" copper tacks

Two 1½" copper nails

One 2" long ¼" zinc eye-bolt
  lag screw

Paint or stain (optional)

Wood filler (optional)

TOOLS

Pencil

Table saw

Miter saw with finish blade

Drill

Screw bit, screw gun, or
  screwdriver

Countersink drill bit

1¼" drill bit

¼" drill bit

Tin snips

Tape measure

Framing square

If you are one of the millions of Americans who enjoy the beauty and sounds of birds, why not promote their well-being by making a summer home for them? Besides providing bird feeders and baths, creating a nesting structure is an important aspect of promoting the return of your favorite backyard summer residents year after year.

The saltbox was a very popular style of home during colonial times, especially in New England. The name stems from the fact that the shape of these homes resembles the boxes used in the seventeenth century to store salt.

Birdhouses are built with particular birds in mind. The entry hole and interior space for this one are customized for attracting black-capped chickadees, although it could be modified for other birds. This house has a closed-off space in the back to provide a properly sized place for the chickadees to nest but could easily be expanded for other birds. The cedar walls and copper roof ensure that the birdhouse will withstand the weather. One wall pivots open so that the birdhouse can be cleaned each spring.

1. Using miter saw, cut 1"×12"×4' into lengths: three 9½", one 6½", and two 4".

2. Create 2 saltbox-shaped sides out of two 9½" pieces. On one 9½" edge, make a mark 4⅝" up from bottom and 8¼" up on other 9½" edge. Place a third mark 3¾" in from the edge with the 8¼" mark and up 10⅜" from bottom. Create the saltbox roof shape by connecting these 3 marks. Cut on lines and use as pattern to trace shape on second 9½" piece. Cut out second saltbox side.

3. Use third 9½" board for rear roof section and front wall of house. Using table saw, cut rear roof section to 6" wide and 9" long, with a 10-degree bevel on top 6" edge (i.e., where roof sections will come together). Cut front wall of house to 4" wide and 8" tall, with a 30-degree bevel along upper 4" edge (i.e., where front wall will meet roof).

4. Use the 6½" length to create front roof section and back wall of house. Cut front roof to 6" wide and 6" long with table saw, with a 15-degree bevel on one end (i.e., where roof sections will come together). Cut back wall of house to 4" wide and 4½" tall, with a 45-degree bevel along upper 4" edge (i.e., where back wall will meet roof).

5. Cut one 4" length to 4"×8⅛" for floor.

6. Create interior divider, by cutting 4" length (from step 1) to a size of 4"×7⅞", with a 45-degree angle cut on upper 4" edge (i.e., where divider will meet roof). Divider is needed to reduce interior space of house to that preferred by chickadees.

7. On one saltbox-shaped side, drill a 1¼" entrance hole 6" up from base of house and 2¾" in from edge.

8. With a ¼" bit, drill 4 drainage holes through the floor, within first 8" of one end.

9. Fasten all pieces together by predrilling, countersinking, and securing with 1⅝" stainless steel screws. Butt front and back walls against inside face of sides. Next, add back wall. Position center divider 8" from side with opening. When attaching front wall, use screws only at top of wall panel in order to create access panel; panel will pivot on screws. Attach floor so that drain holes are in the "occupied" part of house. Finally, attach front and back roof pieces with 1⅝" screws.

10. Drill a ¼" hole through saltbox-shaped side of "unoccupied" part of house (i.e., opposite from side with entrance hole) into edge of front wall. Insert eye-bolt lag screw through side wall into access panel to lock panel shut.

11. With the snips, cut copper flashing into twelve 2"×6" panels and affix to roof with ¾" copper tacks. Predrill holes before nailing through copper and overlap copper panels at least ¾".

12. Leave wood natural, or apply paint or stain. For a more finished look, use wood filler to cover holes.

MATERIALS

One 1"×10"×8' rough-cut pine
    or cedar board
2" stainless steel screws
1¼" stainless steel screws
Exterior wood glue
Waterproof sealer

TOOLS

Miter saw
Drill
¼" drill bit
3" hole saw
Drill bit for pilot holes
Screw bit, screw gun,
    or screwdriver
Countersink bit
Two 18" Quick-Grip clamps
Framing square
Measuring tape
Pencil

This simple owl box, which will provide a home for a family of screech owls or American kestrels, should be set up early in the spring season, when they are looking for a place to nest.

Information on building nest boxes, including materials, designs, and nesting requirements for many species, is readily available on the Internet. Keep in mind that every bird species has its own unique nesting requirements. The diameter of the nest box entrance, size of the box, and placement of the nest box are important factors in successfully attracting a mating pair of any bird species.

This box is built out of one piece of rough-cut pine or cedar and can be made in no time. Wood shavings in the bottom of the box will encourage an owl to nest here and raise its brood. An access panel that can be opened for cleaning is placed on the side, and the box should be cleaned out each year after it has been vacated for the season, so it is ready for the next pair of guests to arrive.

1. Using miter saw, cut two 1¾" strips from end of 1"×10"×8' board. Set strips aside.

2. From the remaining board, use miter saw to cut lengths: one 22" (back of house), three 16" (sides and front), one 12" (roof), and one 7¾" (floor).

3. Use hole saw to make 3" hole on 16" front panel. Center hole on board, 11½" up from bottom edge. These measurements should be customized for whatever bird you are trying to attract.

4. Use ¼" drill bit to make drainage holes in floor of owl house and air holes in sides. Position 4 drainage holes on 7¾" floor panel, 1½" in from corners. Position 2 air holes at the top of both 16" side panels, 1½" in from top corners.

5. Use miter saw to cut 5" off the top and bottom of one 16" side panel. Create access door by trimming the remaining center piece to 5½" long.

6. Position 1¾" strip (from step 1) on top edge of bottom piece of side panel (i.e., piece without air holes), overlapping by ⅞". Clamp, predrill, and countersink screw holes through strip into panel. Unclamp and screw together with 1¼" screws. Attach second 1¾" strip on top edge of access door, overlapping by ⅞".

7. Butt side panel (without door) against rear face of front panel, make edges flush, and clamp together. Ensure panels are square to each other. Drill and countersink pilot holes through front panel into edge of side panel. Unclamp, apply glue, and screw panels together with 1¼" screws. Repeat process to attach assembly to back panel. Position so that back panel extends beyond side panels by 2" at bottom and 4" at top.

8. Attach side with door to owl house. Insert top piece of side (i.e., with air holes) between front panel and back panel. Ensure side edges are flush and top edge aligns with top edge of front panel. Clamp, predrill, and countersink holes into edges from both front panel and back panel. Glue and screw together using 1¼" screws. Repeat process to attach bottom piece of side, ensuring that bottom edge aligns with bottom edge of front panel.

9. Center door in gap in side panel, ensuring edges are flush with ends of front and back panels. The 1¾" strips will align face of door to top and bottom pieces of side panel. Predrill and countersink one hole through front and back panels into top edges of door assembly. In addition to securing door to owl house, these 2" screws will act as pivot points for door to swing inward for cleaning out house.

10. Affix roof and floor panels with glue and 1¼" screws.

Butterfly Observation Cage (page 151)

Watching butterflies in the garden is a wonderful sight and by selecting the right plants, you can ensure that they will not only find the material necessary to make a home in your garden but will have the nectar they need to sustain them.

Nectar-rich plants typically have tubular flowers. In many such plants, the flowers are often held closely together, allowing the butterfly to gather enough nectar from one plant rather than heading off to another spot to search for more. It is important to plant a variety of flowers that will bloom throughout the season so that the butterflies have a source of food for several months. Whether you live in Florida or Minnesota, there are flowers that are hardy to your region and butterflies that are native to your habitat. Some nectar-rich plants to consider are:

Eupatorium pupureum (Joe-Pye weed)
Achillea (yarrow)
Asclepias (milkweed) species
Lindera (spicebush)
Vernonia (ironweed)
Aster species
Aloysia gratissimu (bee bush)

Agastache (hyssop), including the long-blooming cultivar 'Black Adder'
Dalea frutescens (indigo bush)
Echinacea (coneflower)
Rudbeckia (black-eyed Susan)
Mimulus (monkey flowers)
Monarda (bee balm)

Coreopsis (tickseed)
Pycnanthemum (mountain mint) such as 'Cat Springs'
Liatris (gayfeather)
Lantana
Solidago (goldenrod)
Buddleia (butterfly bush) species

In addition, butterflies require a location to go through metamorphosis and need host plants on which to go from being a chrysalis to being a cocoon. Some plants to consider for this are:

Fagus (beech trees)
Cornus (dogwood) species

Aesculus (horse chestnut)
Asclepias (milkweed) species

Lepidopterists have long used observation cages to observe butterflies, but these enclosures can also be used by laypeople to admire these wonderful insects. Once a butterfly is caught in a net, it can be placed in the cage with a nectar-rich plant. After observation, it can be released into the wild by opening the tulle curtain just as if you were stepping out of the shower.

Contrary to popular belief, butterflies are not destroyed by being touched by human hands, although doing so will remove some of their colorful scales.

• *Photograph on page 148*

1. Apply a thin line of glue around outer circle of washer top. Lay tulle square over washer top, stretching it out so tulle is held tautly. Set aside to dry.

2. Lay chain-weight tape out on work surface. Apply a 12- to 14-inch thread of glue along one end of chain weight and use fingers to carry glue to edges. Starting at one end of large piece of tulle, press chain weight to tulle along 65-inch edge. Continue gluing chain-weight tape to tulle until it reaches other corner. Trim excess tape.

3. Cover chain weight on opposite side by gluing twill tape on opposite side of fabric. Set aside to dry for about 5 minutes.

4. After tulle has dried on washer top, use scissors to trim tulle to match outer edge of washer top ring. Next, run a thin line of glue around one-third of metal ring and spread it out with your finger. Starting at top corner of larger piece of tulle (side farthest from chain weights), begin attaching to washer ring. Continue gluing tulle around washer top (tulle should overlap itself by several inches when completely finished).

5. Cut small hole in tulle at the center of washer top, thread loop through hole, and secure with nut on the inside of cage. Attach length of twill tape to loop and hang cage so bottom edge touches ground. A shepherd's hook is ideal for hanging this cage.

6. Place a plant inside cage for butterfly to feed on (see suggestions opposite) and remember to set cage in sun, as butterflies are cold-blooded and like to bask in the sun. Catch a butterfly, sit back, and observe.

MATERIALS AND TOOLS

Clear quick-drying glue, such as Fabri-Tac

One 18-inch washer top (see Note)

A threaded loop and a nut to hang the cage (see Note) to fit washer top

White tulle, enough for a 20-inch square plus a full-width piece 65 inches long

Scissors

2 yards of chain-weight tape (see Note)

2 yards of twill tape the same width as the chain weight—approximately ½ inch wide

Shepherd's hook (optional)

NOTE

Washer tops and the threaded loop can be obtained at lamp-making supply shops. Fabric stores and drapery suppliers carry chain-weight tape.

These pillows bring the inspiration of nature into our homes. Using flowers and butterflies for patterns, ready-made pillow covers can be transformed with hand-dyed fabric and iron-on adhesive for a simple, no-sew project.

MATERIALS AND TOOLS

Liquid fabric dye in several colors (available at craft stores and drugstores)

Natural-fiber pillow cover (cotton, linen, silk, and wool will not melt from the high ironing temperature needed to set adhesive)

About 1 yard white linen

Several large plastic bowls for dyeing (do not reuse for food)

Latex gloves to protect hands from dye

Pressing cloth

Iron and ironing board

Several small swatches of linen to test-dye colors

Double-sided iron-on adhesive, such as Steam-A-Seam 2

Permanent fabric-marking pen (available at fabric and craft stores)

Scissors

1. If using store-bought fabrics, skip steps 1 through 4. If using hand-dyed fabrics, start by cutting white linen into about 8 equal pieces.

2. Dye pieces in a variety of colors to create colored fabric for appliqué patterns. They can be dyed in solid colors or with a gradient of two colors. For a solid color, fill a large plastic bowl with hot tap water, pour a few teaspoons of liquid dye into water, and mix. Thoroughly wet a test swatch of fabric with hot tap water—this will make fabric absorb dye more evenly. Dip swatch in dye; the longer fabric is in dye, the darker it will become. If sample is to your liking, add full panel of fabric. Repeat process with other colors. Rinse out fabric until water runs clear and hang to dry.

3. To dye fabric two colors, have two dye baths ready at same time. Wet fabric with hot water. Dip only half fabric piece in first dye bath and dip other half into second dye bath. Let color wick up fabric slightly until it meets first color. You can also leave a white space between the two colors, or overlap the colors to create a third color in the center of the fabric piece. Rinse out fabric until water runs clear and hang to dry. Dye several pieces of fabric so that you have a selection to work with when you begin appliquéing.

4. Cut off a piece of double-sided iron-on adhesive to about the same size as fabric pieces. Peel off paper backing on one side. Place dyed fabric on tacky side of adhesive sheet. Repeat with all of your fabric.

5. Draw desired patterns on paper side of the iron-on adhesive. Cut out all the patterns for your pillow. Arrange pattern on pillow to your liking.

6. Heat iron to high setting. Peel off paper backings of pattern pieces and rearrange them on pillow cover. Place a pressing cloth over appliqué pieces. Press pieces down, following manufacturer's instructions for iron-on adhesive.

7. Use a permanent fabric-marking pen to draw in further embellishments on your patterns, such as flower stems or other details.

MUSHROOM WOOD BAT HOUSE

MATERIALS

Cypress or hemlock
    mushroom wood:
One 1"×8"×8' board, planed
One 1"×8"×6' board, 1 inch
    by 8 inches, brushed (more
    rustic look)
1½" and 1¼" stainless steel
    shank nails
Fiberglass screening
⅜" staples
Translucent exterior caulking

TOOLS

Table saw
Miter saw
Tape measure
Hammer
Staple gun
Pencil
Scissors

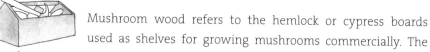

Mushroom wood refers to the hemlock or cypress boards used as shelves for growing mushrooms commercially. The mushrooms grow in a sterilized substrate laid directly on the shelves. As the mushrooms grow, they produce an enzyme that eats away at the soft tissue of the wood, leaving behind the most durable and rot-resistant part of the wood. Periodically the shelves are replaced and the old wood—with its unique and beautiful patina—is used for furniture, paneling, and other building projects.

Not only is recycled wood, such as the mushroom wood used here, beautiful and environmentally friendly, it also increases the odds of luring bats to live in a bat house. If your initial reaction to attracting bats to the backyard isn't positive, keep in mind that bats are an excellent way to reduce mosquito populations. And because they are primarily nocturnal, they do the work while you sleep.

Attracting bats is a mixture of know-how and luck. Bats like to live in a relatively small enclosed space that will help capture their body heat. They prefer to enter through a small opening in the base of the structure. Heat is an important factor in bats' choosing to move into a bat house. In areas where the average summer temperature is below 85 degrees F., a bat house should face south or southwest to take advantage of the warm sunlight. Where the average summer temperature is above 85 degrees, a bat house should be positioned in a more northerly direction and out of direct sunlight. Bat houses are best placed away from your house. Ideally, use an outbuilding, such as a garage or barn, and hang the bat house at least 15 feet aboveground.

This project can also easily be made with other kinds of lumber.

1. Cut planed 1"×8"×8' board into four 15½" lengths and two 22" lengths.

2. Create back wall of bat house, 15½" wide × 24¾" tall: Use table saw to rip down 15½" lengths into three 6" widths. Set blade of table saw to 15-degree bevel to rip fourth board into a 6¾" width, to accept pitch of roof.

3. Return table saw blade to 90 degrees and set blade to ⅛" depth. Make a series of grooves lengthwise on bottom 3" of one 15½"×6" board to serve as a landing pad for bats to cling to. Space grooves ¼" apart. This board will be the bottommost board on the back wall, with grooves at bottom. Use table saw to rip down 22" piece into three 1½" widths and one 1" width. Set aside 1" board.

4. Using miter saw, create side walls of bat house by cutting a 15-degree angle on one end of 2 of the 1½"×22" pieces. Cut other ends at right angles to create two 21½" lengths.

5. Place side walls on work surface parallel and about 15½" apart. Position the back sides of the 4 boards of back wall on side walls. Line up beveled edge of top board with angled edge of side walls. Position "landing pad" grooves at the bottom of the back wall facing toward the front. Sides of bat house will be shy of bottom edge of back wall, leaving the grooves exposed. While attaching pieces together, apply thin layer of caulk between boards to waterproof seams and fasten the back boards to the side walls with 1½" shank nails.

6. Use miter saw to cut one 1½"×22" board to a length of 14", for the interior ceiling. Turn structure over and attach ceiling to top of back wall, just below the lowest point of side wall angles. Fasten with 1½" nails, using a thick layer of caulk, to waterproof structure.

7. Using scissors, cut a piece of screening to roughly fit interior of bat house. Use ⅜" staples to attach a piece of fiberglass screening to the inside of the back wall. Screening will provide a surface for the bats to hang from once inside the house.

8. Install front panels. Use miter saw to cut brushed 1"×8"×6' board into 4 lengths of 15½". Use table saw to rip 3 panels into widths that will cover entire face of house and stop flush with bottom edge of side walls, leaving grooved overhang exposed. Bevel top panel 15 degrees along its top edge to line up with roofline. Position boards on house, caulk, and fasten top 2 boards of the front wall.

9. Use miter saw to cut remaining 1"×22" piece (from step 4) into a 14" length. Set table saw blade to 45 degrees and create bevel on 1" side. Fasten this piece to inside bottom center of remaining board for front wall, so that it will fit snugly between the two side walls when the third board is attached to the front. Make sure that the bevel will face up when the third front board is attached.

10. Position third front board on face of bat house, creating a ¾" opening for bats to enter on underside, above the grooved landing pad. Caulk and fasten with nails.

11. Create roof by ripping down the final remaining brushed board to 5" wide with a 15-degree bevel on the top edge. Caulk and fasten to top of bat house using 1¼" nails. Hang in the appropriate location (see headnote).

HOME

Just as birds build nests and bees build hives, we create our own safe havens from which we can observe the world. And whether we are building a simple garden shed, crafting handmade furniture that makes life more comfortable, or screening a door to keep the mosquitoes away, home improvement projects provide us with a way of making a mark on the world we inhabit. Even our favorite pets understand the pride of home ownership.

Adventurous weekend carpenters with the time and skill to build a custom doghouse from scratch have a wide array of building plans to choose from. Remodeling a standard stock doghouse can produce a similar custom look. Before you choose which way to go, there are a number of things to consider so that you can provide your best friend with a retreat from the heat and shelter from the rain.

First and foremost, select an appropriate size house for the breed of dog. A house too small will not be a comfortable place in which to lie down and relax. One that's too big will not allow the pet's own body heat to maintain a comfortable temperature inside the doghouse. A good rule of thumb is to select a house that allows the dog to stand upright, turn around, and lie down comfortably.

Bedding material should be limited to wood shavings or a 1"-thick rubber mat often used in horse stables (this material is soft on the pet's feet but easy to wash down with a hose). Stay away from blankets or fiber-filled beds, which can get wet and moldy and, in colder temperatures, freeze (stiff, frozen blankets are not comfortable to rest on).

Insulate the house to contain the heat generated by your pet in colder climates and to keep the heat out in hot climates. Styrofoam panels in the rafters provide the same sort of insulating protection that's found in most homes. These panels are inexpensive, light, easy to cut to size, and wedge in nicely between the roof supports of the doghouse. If the roof is to be shingled, the Styrofoam also acts as a protective barrier for the nails that will protrude through the underside of the roof.

Consider location when placing a doghouse. The door should not face in the direction of prevailing winds, and the house should be in a shady area in the summer and a sunny location in the winter. Under that large deciduous tree in the backyard may be the ideal spot!

Now that the house is suitable for the dog, the fun part is to make it an attractive addition to the yard. Be creative and mimic design elements and features from the main house or a garden shed to make the house look as if it belongs there.

As with any home or outbuilding, keeping the doghouse protected from the elements is important, and using the proper exterior materials will maximize the life of the structure.

Roofing materials such as cedar or asphalt shingles and metal are all good choices. In the doghouse pictured (page 156), we cut down cedar shingles to a smaller size to keep the look of the house in scale with the overall size of the structure.

As with the roofing materials, the options for sidewall materials are numerous. Cedar shingles, aluminum siding, and clapboard are probably the most popular choices. Clapboard was our choice—here, we ripped down 2×4 cedar boards on a table saw into ¼"-thick pieces and overlapped them onto the sides of the house, fastening them with stainless steel screws. Be sure that the interior walls have some type of protective sheathing to conceal the nail ends that will protrude into the interior of the doghouse.

Additional decorative features include faux windows. To build the windows, cut down ¼" exterior-grade plywood to the preferred window size and paint the plywood black with an exterior-grade paint. Cut down small strips of wood for the window trim and to create the appearance of individual windowpanes. Glue these pieces into place and attach with nails from the back side. With a few finish nails, attach the windows to the walls.

Think about adding a secure front door. This often overlooked feature helps ensure that the only animal living in the doghouse is the one for which it was built. Opening the door on days when the dog is out and leaving it closed on days the dog is inside will discourage any uninvited guests from taking up residence. (Evicting a skunk is not an enjoyable task!)

In the end, if your pet still enjoys the comfort of your house over its own doghouse, at least you will have something aesthetically pleasing to look at in the yard. • *Photograph on page 156*

Porch swings make taking it easy with family and friends on summer evenings a sublime experience. This child-sized version is perfect for creating a place for any child to sit and read a book or relax with a favorite stuffed animal. Because it's small, it fits on even a tiny back porch or under the eaves of a house. Although the end result looks as if it might be beyond the average woodworker's skills, it is surprisingly simple to assemble once all the pieces have been cut out. The template for the seat and backrest of the swing can easily be roughed out on cardboard, traced onto the lumber, and cut with a jigsaw.

1. Review the diagram and draw the outline of a seat support, backrest support, and armrest onto cardboard. Cut out shapes with sharp utility knife to create templates.

2. Outline 3 seat and backrest supports by copying template (see page 162) onto one of the 2"×4"×8' boards. Cut out pieces with jigsaw, sand, and attach one seat support to each backrest support using glue and 3" stainless steel screws. Trace armrests, cut out, and sand smooth.

3. Use table saw to rip 1"×10"×10' board into six 1½" strips. Use miter saw to cut strips into sixteen 40" seat slats. Use remaining wood to cut three 39" slats.

4. Use miter saw to cut 2"×4"×8' into two 39" bottom support rails.

5. Use table saw and miter saw to create two 1½"×2⅝"×8¾" arm uprights.

6. Position the 3 seat and backrest supports on bottom support rails, one on each end and the third in center. From the underside, predrill and countersink holes for screws. Secure with 3" stainless steel screws.

7. Align an arm upright with the front bottom support rail on each side. The 2⅝" face should be flat against the support rail. Predrill, countersink, and secure with 2½" stainless steel screws.

8. Position armrests on uprights. Inside edge of armrest should be flush with inside face of upright arm support. Overhang front of armrest 1½" beyond front of upright. Predrill screw holes and countersink for screws. Secure armrest to upright with 2" wood screws. To attach rear end of armrests to back supports, predrill hole through outermost back supports into edge of each armrest and secure with lag bolts.

9. Attach seat slats, starting at the crook of seat and back. Predrill, countersink, and secure each slat to each support with a 2½" screw. Slats will overhang end supports. Use 3 shorter slats at armrest uprights. Similarly, attach backrest slats.

[CONTINUED]

MATERIALS

Two 2"×4"×8' cedar boards

Two 1"×10"×10' cedar boards

2½" stainless steel wood screws

3" stainless steel wood screws

25' heavy chain

Two ¼"×3" galvanized lag bolts

Six 2" chain connectors

Four 5/16"×6" eye-bolt lag screws

Cardboard for templates

Exterior-grade wood glue

TOOLS

Table saw

Miter saw with finish blade

Jigsaw

Belt sander

Drill

Screw bit, screw gun, or screwdriver

⅞" wood-boring bit

Drill bit for pilot holes

Countersink bit

Pilot drill bit

Utility knife

Tape measure

Framing square

Pencil

Glue

NOTE

All hardware and chain must be rated to support more than the estimated weight of the swing and occupants.

Porch swing detail

10. Mark locations for chain holes through armrests. Position front hole 3" from front of armrest and ¾" from outside edge. Position rear hole 1½" from rear end of armrest and centered on armrest. Drill 4 holes using ⅞" wood-boring bit.

11. Mark location for eye-bolt lag screws (for attaching chains) ¾ inch from bottom of front and rear bottom support rails, in line with holes through armrests. Predrill and attach eye-bolt lag screws on both sides of swing.

12. Install hooks into ceiling joist or beam and attach chains between hooks and eye-bolt lag screws, through holes in armrests. Adjust chain length until swing is balanced. Seat height should be comfortable for getting onto and off swing yet high enough to keep feet from dragging on the ground.

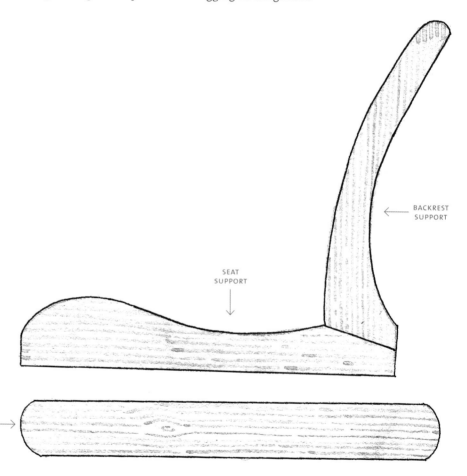

Porch swing template

A waist-high table at the back door will be useful every day—a spot to put groceries down when fumbling for keys, to set out lemonade for the kids on a summer afternoon, and to display flowering plants. When this pair of wrought-iron gates was uncovered at a local salvage yard, it was clear that, with the addition of a precut bluestone step or concrete paver as a tabletop, it could make a perfect table.

While the welding in this project may be beyond most do-it-yourselfers, a local blacksmith can help to connect the two pieces together with a little welding and some cold steel. Another idea for the base is an old flat-topped radiator, which doesn't require welding but would still be a welcome resting place for packages at your back door.

MATERIALS

1 roll of fiberglass screening

A length of medium-weight
cotton fabric at least
4 inches longer than
the height of your door
opening

Thread to match fabric

Drapery chain-weight tape
(see Notes)

TOOLS

Scissors

Sewing machine

Iron and ironing board

Hand sewing needle

Pencil

Grommet tool (see Notes)

NOTES

Chain-weight tape can be
obtained at fabric and
drapery stores.

Grommets can also be put
in professionally at many
fabric stores.

Everyone gets tired of hearing the screen door open and close in good weather. This screen allows silent movement in and out of the house without letting the bugs in. Cats and dogs love this screen because it allows them to come and go as they please. A similar version can be made for unscreened windows and just held in place on all four sides for a screened-in-porch effect.

Stripes look great as a border of the screen, and they provide an easy guide to cut on. None of the sewing required is complex, but if it seems like too much for you, coerce a crafty friend into helping.

1. Using scissors, cut fiberglass screening to a size 2 inches wider and 2 inches longer than the size of the door opening for which it is being made.

2. Cut two strips 8 inches wide from your cotton fabric equal in length to the length of the screen.

3. Cut two strips 8 inches wide from your cotton fabric that measure 3 inches longer than the width of the screen.

4. Lay the cotton strips wrong side up on work surface or ironing board. Fold each long side in so that it meets the center of strip—the 2 long sides should be parallel down the middle of the strip. Using iron, press the long sides of the cotton strips in so that they just meet in the center. Fold over in half again and press with iron to form a finished binding strip. Repeat with remaining strips.

5. Set out one of the long strips and open in half like a book. Lay long edge of fiberglass screening onto the cotton strip so the screen edge butts up to the center fold in the cotton strip. Close the cotton strip, sandwiching the screen inside it.

6. With needle and thread to match your fabric, baste the folded cotton strip to the screen about ¼ inch from the inner edge of the binding. Repeat steps 5 and 6 on opposite long side of the screening with remaining long strip.

7. Lay shorter strip over top of screening in the same manner as the long sides were set. Center the cotton strip on the screen, leaving a 1½" overhang on both sides. To remove some fabric bulk from corners, trim away the inner fold of the cotton strip back to the width of the screen. Repeat on opposite side of strip.

8. Remove folded cotton strip from the end of the screen. Fold and press ends of folded cotton strip. Re-press the centerfold of the folded cotton strip. Sandwich the end of the screen inside strip as before and baste strip to screening.

9. Baste a length of chain-weight tape on bottom edge of screen, leaving a 2-inch strip on each end without weights to avoid running into them when finishing edge on the sewing machine. Bind and baste the remaining end of the screen (repeat steps 7 and 8).

10. Using a sewing machine, stitch the inside edge of the 2 long sides back, stitching at the beginning and end of each stitch line.

11. Stitch the inside edge of the 2 short sides back, stitching at the beginning and end of each stitch line.

12. Mark the unweighted end of the screen for 3 grommet holes—one at each end (about ¾ inch in) and one in the center of the top edge. Use a grommet tool to attach grommets or have the grommets professionally done at a local fabric store.

13. Hang the screen on 3 nails or hooks in the door frame.

STOCK SHED

Stock sheds have been a boon for the storage-challenged gardener or backyard craftsman. By retrofitting a prefab shed with salvaged windows and some shingle siding, you can easily add a seasonal sitting room or home office to the backyard for a lot less money than an addition to the house.

MATERIALS

One 1"×12"×8' pine board
One 1"×10"×8' pine board
2" wood screws
Four #10 brass wood screws,
 1½" long
Exterior wood glue
2' length of ⅜" wood dowel

TOOLS

Table saw
Miter saw with finish blade
Jigsaw
Drill
Countersink drill bit
⅜" drill bit
Screw bit, screw gun,
 or screwdriver
Tape measure
Framing square
Sanding block or palm sander
Fine-grade sandpaper
Pencil
Two 36" Quick-Grip clamps
Coping saw

 From work and picnic benches to bleacher seats at a ball game, the bench is an iconic product of woodworkers. Whether placed near the door as a place to catch shoes, baseball mitts, and the occasional bag of groceries as you're unlocking the door, or in pairs around a table for an impromptu picnic, this classic bench will find a use in any backyard. While these benches are common, the details on this one—the arches on the legs, the angled ends on the seat rails, and the angled leg supports under the seat—show a level of craftsmanship that will leave any do-it-yourselfer feeling proud of the result.

1. Use miter saw to cut 1"×12"×8' board to 72". Set aside short piece. Rip down 72" length with table saw to create seat 10¾" wide.

2. Use miter saw to cut 1"×10"×8' board to 68". Set aside short piece. Rip down 68" length with table saw to make 2 underside support rails each 3" wide. Set miter saw blade to 45 degrees and cut a decorative angle on ends of both rails. Start cut 1¼" down from the top edge of rail.

3. Use leftover board stock to make 2 legs, each 17¼"×9¼".

4. Use jigsaw to make notches at the top of both sides of legs, ¾" wide by 3" tall. Rails will sit on these notches.

5. Create arch detail at the bottom of both legs. Start and end of arch will be 1½" from the outer edges of the leg. Center of arch will be 2½" up from bottom of leg. Draw arch connecting these 3 points. Use jigsaw to cut out arch.

6. Create angled supports between seat bottom and inside of leg, composed of a vertical base, horizontal base, and angled cross brace. Use remaining pine stock to create the following pieces: two 8¼"×3" pieces (vertical bases), two 9"×3" pieces (horizontal bases), and two 6¾"×6¾" pieces (cross braces). Using table saw, chamfer at a 45-degree angle two face edges of 8¼" sides and one adjoining 3" side of the 8¼" pieces. Starting 2" down from the top edge, add a 45-degree angle to cross braces (6¾"×6¾") by using miter saw to remove the corner of each 6¾" square.

7. Assemble angled supports and secure with wood glue and countersunk 2" screws, predrilling holes in pieces to prevent splitting. Butt unchamfered 3" edge of 8¼" vertical base to the 3" end of the 9" horizontal base to create a 90-degree angle. Chamfered edges will be on the inside of the 90" corner. Inside the corner, attach the 6¾" angled cross brace, centered on the 2 bases.

8. With seat facedown, dry-fit rails and legs. Position rails 2" in from both ends of seat and ¾" in from sides. Position legs 6" in from each end with rails sitting flush in notches on legs.

9. Use framing square to ensure legs are plumb (i.e., 90 degrees from seat bottom) and square to rails. Drill pilot holes, countersink, and screw rails to legs using 3 screws on each leg. Install angled supports in between the underside of the seat and the inside of the legs, drill four pilot holes, countersink, and attach with $1\frac{1}{2}$" brass wood screws.

10. Carefully flip the bench over and clamp seat to rails. Mark screw locations $1\frac{1}{8}$" in from the side of the seat for fastening the seat to rails at (from end) $3\frac{1}{2}$", $10\frac{1}{2}$", 1'11$\frac{1}{2}$", 3', 4$\frac{1}{2}$", 4'10", and 5'8$\frac{1}{2}$". Make a mark $6\frac{3}{8}$" from each end, centered on the seat (i.e., $5\frac{3}{8}$" from the edge), where wood screws will fasten the seat to legs. At all marked locations, drill pilot holes, countersink screw heads, and secure with 2" screws.

11. Cut dowels to create plugs and use wood glue to plug all screw holes on seat face, cut flush with coping saw, and sand. Apply finish of choice.

MATERIALS AND TOOLS

Unfinished furniture for painting

Milk paint (a good brand is the Old Fashioned Milk Paint Company)

Paint stirrer

Warm water

Resealable containers

Cheesecloth or nylon stocking (optional)

Paintbrush

Fine-grade sandpaper

Environmentally friendly water-resistant sealer such as Aqua Resin Stain Finish by Bioshield

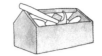

The use of milk paint dates back many thousands of years. Examples have been found in early cave paintings as well as in Egyptian tombs. Because of its simple formula (milk protein, lime, and earth pigments), it has been a staple in decoration throughout history, and it works well in bringing unfinished furniture to life.

Milk paint is known for its beautiful muted colors and matte finish, but it is also nontoxic, solvent free, and very easy to use. One of its few drawbacks is that it is not water resistant, but earth-friendly sealers can resolve this issue with almost as little impact on the environment as nontoxic milk paint.

1. Choose an item to paint with an unfinished wood surface. Lightly sand its surface, if necessary. Milk paint will penetrate into clean porous unfinished surfaces without needing any primer. The surface of dried milk paint has a flat, slightly uneven or grainy appearance that creates an antique-looking finish.

2. Mix milk paint, following manufacturer's instructions. For a small project, mix paint by hand in a wide-mouthed resealable container, so your paintbrush will fit and the container can be covered between coats. For larger projects (requiring 1 gallon of paint or more), use a wire paint paddle attachment on your drill to mix the paint. In container, gradually add small amounts of warm water and dry pigment to make a paste. Mix until smooth. Continue to add equal amounts of warm water and pigment until you have desired amount of paint. If you have small lumps, strain the paint through cheesecloth or a nylon stocking. Let the paint stand 10 to 15 minutes before using, to let the ingredients evenly disperse.

3. Apply 2 to 3 coats of paint, with good-quality brush. Let item dry completely between each coat and lightly sand before applying next coat.

4. If you like, try layering different colors and sanding through the top layer to reveal the colors below.

5. Apply water-resistant coating to protect the paint's surface from water-spotting.

MILK GLASS LUMINARIAS
Nothing sets off the evening better than the glow of candles casting their shadows across the landscape. When we happened on an array of vintage milk glass vases and glassware used as votives, we knew that we had discovered a new use for these easy-to-find collectibles. Buying an array of shapes and sizes and using them to house tea lights allows their forms to take on a sculptural quality.

 Old-fashioned clotheslines not only remind us of freshly washed sheets smelling of the outdoors and of playing in the backyard as children but, with the rising cost of energy and concerns about global warming, reduce our energy footprint on the environment. Making one that also serves as a trellis for flowering vines, affords a welcome sight even when it's not in use.

We use cedar posts to build the two crosses that support the drying lines. These posts give the structure some presence, which helps make it an architectural feature in the backyard. Diagonal guide wires are strung on each cross post for clematis or morning glories that may even trail out onto the clothesline itself. A bit of lavender or rosemary planted underneath the posts might also help freshen laundry further. These posts can safely be set about 18 feet apart. If more lines are needed, consider adding a center post.

1. Using miter saw, cut one post into two 4' sections.

2. Chamfer top of two 8' posts and both ends of two 4' sections by setting miter saw to a 30-degree bevel and trimming away post ends on all 4 sides, 1" from top.

3. Create half lap joints to connect posts and arms. Notch out both 8' posts 3" from the top of the chamfer to accept the 4' cross section. Set depth of circular saw blade to $\frac{1}{2}$ the thickness of post. Make a series of close cuts in notch area that is to be removed. Use chisel to clean out resulting "fingers" of wood. Remove a section $1\frac{1}{2}$" deep by $3\frac{1}{2}$" wide (the actual dimension of the 4×4 post). Use same process to notch out both 4' sections at their centers. Remove notch $1\frac{1}{2}$" deep by $3\frac{1}{2}$" wide.

4. At notches, overlap 8' post and 4' arm and clamp together. Predrill two $\frac{3}{8}$" holes on a diagonal at the joint, secure with two 4" carriage bolts, washers, and nuts, and remove clamps.

5. Mark 3 locations on arm for clotheslines. Center first line position at center of post connection and space 2 remaining positions 6" from ends of arm.

6. Mark locations for trellis wires. On underside of both ends of cross section, center a mark 1" from end; center 4 more marks 4" apart. On the post face underneath each arm, make a mark 66" down from cross post and then space 4 marks every $13\frac{1}{2}$" up post.

[CONTINUED]

MATERIALS

Three 4"×4"×8' cedar posts
Four $\frac{3}{8}$" carriage bolts, 4" long
Four sets washers and nuts, to match carriage bolts
Forty-six #208 zinc-plated eye hooks
Fifty-two $\frac{1}{8}$"" galvanized clamps
Twenty $\frac{5}{32}$"×$4\frac{3}{4}$" galvanized turnbuckle eye hooks
75' of $\frac{1}{8}$" braided galvanized wire
Six $\frac{3}{16}$""×5' galvanized turnbuckle eye hooks
65' of $\frac{1}{8}$" vinyl-coated braided galvanized wire
Concrete
Gravel (optional)

TOOLS

Circular saw
Miter saw with finish blade
Drill
Chisel
$\frac{3}{8}$" and $\frac{1}{8}$" drill bits
Framing square
Tape measure
Clamps
$\frac{9}{16}$" socket wrench
Rotary tool such as a Dremel
Metal-cutting disk for rotary tool
Post-hole digger or shovel
Level
Pencil

7. Predrill all 20 marks with ⅛" drill bit. Screw eye hooks into each hole.

8. Starting with innermost set of trellis eye hooks, attach uncoated braided wire with ⅛" galvanized clamps and 5/32" turnbuckles. Use rotary tool to cut off excess wire. Turnbuckles should be positioned on post end of wire. Repeat with other support.

9. Select site for installation. Posts should be set parallel to each other about 12 to 18' apart. Using a post hole digger or shovel, dig holes for supports. The supports should be set 2' into the ground, level and even with each other. The posts should be held in place with gravel and can be reinforced with concrete.

10. Using ⅛" clamps and 5" turnbuckle eye hooks, attach 3 lengths of the vinyl-coated wire between the 2 supports. Use a turnbuckle at both ends of each clothesline to make line taut.

The guy wires on the lines can easily be tightened by twisting the turnbuckles

Stilted or pleached hedges in the garden have been a tradition for centuries, but this miniature topiary version is ideal for anyone who doesn't have room for the real thing. These attractive miniature hedges make wonderful centerpieces and would be ideal as a take-home centerpiece for a shower or wedding.

1. Select 3 standards (a shrub or herb trained to grow with one straight main stem, like that of a tree, such as coleus, *Eugenia,* myrtle, boxwood, or *Santolina*) from a local nursery or garden center. Find a long, narrow container large enough to hold the plants in a row—a window-box-shaped container is ideal.

2. Plant the 3 hedges in the container in a straight row, filling in around each with good-quality potting mix.

3. Stake each plant with a bamboo or thin wood stake and tie loosely to the trunk with raffia.

4. Tie the stakes of the 3 topiaries to a bamboo stake running perpendicular to their trunks.

5. Trim the plants back with pruners and begin to shape them into a single rectangular hedge, using the edge of the pot as a guide. Keep in mind that wherever you cut, the plant will put out 2 branches and thicken. Hedges like these need continual pruning to look good.

6. Water in the hedge. If you like, plant a ground cover such as baby's tears at the hedge's base.

MATERIALS

3 standards or topiaries
Oblong planter
Potting mix
Twine or raffia
Bamboo
Ground cover (optional)

TOOLS

Scissors
Pruners

MATERIALS AND TOOLS

Broken terra-cotta pot,
    preferably with just 1 or
    2 clean breaks
Pencil
Single-ply copper wire
Rotary tool such as a Dremel
⅛" masonry drill bit
Wire cutters

In our disposable culture we sometimes forget that there is a beauty in items that have been well used and are then given a second chance through repair. For example, an old terra-cotta pot can be repaired quickly and easily, using nothing more than some copper wire and a masonry bit. This technique, which can give a favorite old pot a bit of character, is also a great way to repair a hairline crack before it becomes more severe.

1. Fit broken piece of terra-cotta pot into place. Using pencil, mark pot to determine where to drill. The marks should be placed like holes for laces on a sneaker (about ¼ to ½ inch in from break to prevent terra-cotta from cracking when drilled). The copper wire will be strung through holes and tightened to hold piece in place.

2. Use rotary tool fitted with masonry bit to drill holes on either side of the crack.

3. Cut wire into 3-inch lengths. From the outside of pot, put wire length halfway through bottom drill hole on pot and put other end through bottommost hole of broken piece. Twist copper wires together inside pot and trim excess wire. Repeat on remaining pairs of holes. Push twisted copper wire against pot until flush with pot.

TERRA-COTTA CHIMNEY POT
Terra-cotta chimney pots are
still made today and can often
be found in architectural salvage
and junk yards as well. Their
earthy tones fit in anywhere, and
they have a multitude of uses in
the garden and on the terrace.
Here, a chimney pot serves as
a pedestal to highlight a plant
in the middle of the perennial
border. Other uses include as
camouflage for outdoor lighting
(covered versions take on the
appearance of a lantern); in a
pair as the base of a potting
bench or a serving table, with the
addition of a wooden tabletop
(create plywood cutouts to fit
into chimney pot tops and attach
to tabletop to stabilize table, if
needed); and as a rhubarb forcer
(see page 40).

WATER

Essential to all forms of life, water mesmerizes us with its shimmering surfaces and the way it catches light. Throughout time, water has been coveted and, though we have taken access to it for granted in the past century or so, our reverence for water seems to be taking on a new life as we recognize the importance of this precious resource and the beauty it can help foster.

Containerized water gardens make beautiful focal points for decks and patios and can be kept anywhere there is an ample amount of sun.

The basic requirements are the container and the plants. It's very simple to build your own containerized water garden. Options for plants include floaters, such as water lettuce and water hyacinths, which sit atop the water's surface with their roots dangling in the water; marginals such as *Equisetum, Alocasia,* cannas, and papyrus, whose crowns (where the roots meet the stems) sit above the water with their roots planted below the water's surface; or bottom rooters, such as water lilies and lotus, which prefer to have their roots and crowns planted in soil underwater with their leaves and flowers pushing up just above the water's surface.

The growing popularity of water gardening has led to a plethora of water plants being available both locally and through the mail. The amount and type of plants and the potential addition of fish to your water garden depend on the size and depth of the container. Apart from the occasional feeding of the plants and fish, these gardens require minimal care and should need no more than topping off with additional fresh water from time to time.

1. Select your site. Make sure the location has at least 4 hours of direct sun each day. Most water plants want an adequate amount of light in order to stay healthy and produce flowers.

2. Choose a container. The larger the container, the more choices you will have for both plants and fish. Any waterproof container will do—for both floaters and submerged plants, a container as big as a half-sized barrel or larger is optimal. The larger volume of water helps prevent the water temperature from fluctuating too much from day to night. Keep in mind that if you choose a large container such as a half whiskey barrel, it will be too heavy to move once filled with water. Marginals are more forgiving of the container's size than floaters or bottom rooters.

3. Add water. If the water is chlorinated (as is most tap water unless it is drawn from a well), fill the container and let the water sit untouched for several days to allow the chlorine to dissipate before adding plants.

4. Set in the plants. Most water plants come in plastic bags to keep them from drying out. For floaters, simply remove the plants from the bag and place them on the surface of the water, making sure their roots are submerged. For bottom rooters, such as dwarf water lilies or lotus, simply place the plant's pot 1 to 2 feet below the surface of the water for water lilies and no less than 6 inches beneath

the water's surface for a lotus. If your container is deeper, use bricks or cinder blocks to elevate the plant to the appropriate height (the planting instructions will usually list a suggested depth for setting each plant). Repot marginal plants into terra-cotta pots and water well. Place the pot in the water-filled container so that the bottom few inches of the clay pot are submerged but the crown is above the waterline. Cannas can be grown this way with spectacular results.

5. If the container is large (more than 18 inches deep and 48 inches wide), you can add a few goldfish. Goldfish are easy to care for and will help keep the water garden free of mosquitoes. Goldfish prefer to live in water that is not too hot, so make sure your plants keep the water shaded and cool. This will also prevent algae from growing. An aerator can be added to increase the supply of oxygen to the fish and will create a nice sound effect as well, although in a container as large as a whiskey barrel, an aerator is not necessary. Another way of preventing mosquito larvae is to add a mosquito dunk every month. These mosquito dunks, or Bt rings, deliver *Bacillus thuringiensis,* an organic control that stops the development of mosquito larvae.

Bog plants have a beauty all their own and are perfect for planting out in a container. Since they prefer waterlogged soil to the point just below their crowns (where the roots meet the stem), they can be lower maintenance than traditional container plants because they don't dry out as quickly.

Many waterproof containers without a drainage hole can be used to create a bog garden. A bog is an area that has standing water most of the year and is composed of decayed plant material under the surface. There aren't many nutrients in a bog, so plants that grow in them don't require very fertile soil. Carnivorous plants, such as Venus flytraps, butterworts, and pitcher plants *(Sarracenia),* get their nutrition from digesting bugs and therefore often can grow in bogs. The planting process is simple and straightforward.

1. Select a container that will hold water.

2. Soak enough peat moss to fill container with water for several hours or overnight.

3. Mound the peat moss and create a dome-shaped mass in the container. This will help show the plants to their best effect and ensure that the crowns of the plants are above the waterline.

4. Plant the mound out with the species suggested above, setting their crowns (where the roots meet the stems) just at the surface of the peat moss.

5. Add live spaghnum moss around the top and water in well.

6. Keep well watered throughout the season. As these plants do not typically get their nutrition from the soil, there is no need to fertilize regularly.

Besides providing water for birds, a birdbath can also provide water for marginal plants. Marginals are plants that like their roots wet but their crowns (where the roots meet the stems) dry. Simply plant a marginal (see list below) in a clay pot with a drainage hole, set plant in center of birdbath, and fill birdbath with water. Most marginals prefer full sun, so set birdbath in a sunny site. Top off water regularly and tip out bath and refill with fresh water from time to time to prevent algae from growing. There is still room for the birds to bathe and the plants require a less demanding watering schedule than would otherwise be necessary.

Some marginals to consider:

Cannas	Variegated *Acorus*	Plantain lilies
Horsetails *(Equisetum)*	(sweet flag)	Dwarf papyrus
Japanese iris	Corkscrew rush	Taro or *Alocasia*

Gilt objects call to mind ornate mirrors, but gilding has long been used for its ornamental quality outdoors—from signage to the domes of capitol buildings—and can hold back the elements for decades. So why not give a flea market find such as these vintage lily pad tables a bit of glamour with the addition of some silver or gold leaf? With three holes drilled into its base on an angle, a gold-leafed finial becomes an elegant tripod on which to grow morning glories. Once the art of gilding is mastered, you may even decide to go for the impossible and gild a lily—or at least the seed head of a lotus. Practice on a spare surface before starting, to get a sense of the process. • *Photograph on page 186*

MATERIALS

Furniture or object for gilding
High-gloss spray paint
Sheets of silver patent leaf or
    gold patent leaf
Quick Size (3-hour) varnish
Clear polyurethane

TOOL

Fine-grade sandpaper
Squirrel-hair artist's brush

1. Any surface can accept leaf if it is nonporous, but surface preparation is important because irregularities will transfer through the leaf. Make the surface smooth by sanding lightly with very fine sandpaper, then use high-gloss spray paint to seal the surface and make it glossy. After prepping surface, avoid handling painted surface so as not to transfer oil from hands.

2. Select a cool, shady, draft-free location to work in. Using a soft brush, lay a thin, even layer of Quick Size on surface to be gilded.

3. Check the tack of the sized object after about 20 to 30 minutes by pressing the back of a knuckle to the surface. It should not feel sticky when knuckle is pulled away, but there should be a slight pull accompanied by a faint clicking sound; this is known as the tack. If the sizing is too wet, it will come through the leaf. If it is too dry, the leaf will not stick. Tack time will vary depending on weather conditions. Sizing will set more quickly on a dry day, while humidity will slow it down.

4. When the surface has come to tack, begin leafing. On a flat surface, an entire sheet can be used at one time. For convex or concave areas, tear the leaf into small pieces. Leaf does not cut well with scissors but is easily torn by hand. Remove one piece of the leaf with backing paper attached. Press it lightly but firmly onto surface. Avoid touching surrounding sized areas. Carefully remove the paper (fingerprints translate through gold leaf). Pick up another piece of leaf. Lay it down slightly overlapping the edge of the first one. Continue until the piece is covered in leaf.

5. Additional layers may be added after the leaf has been allowed to set. Silver leaf needs a clear coat to protect it from tarnishing, but gold leaf will not tarnish. However, for a surface that will get wear and tear (such as these tabletops), a clear coat of polyurethane protects gold leaf.

Water-Gilding a Lily Pad Table (page 185)

RAIN LILIES

Rain lilies have an ephemeral beauty that makes them much loved in the South. These heat- and drought-tolerant bulbs make a wonderful planting in a bowl with decorative mulch (bulbs are set in plastic pots underneath the mulch) and come into bloom shortly after they receive a nice rain.

RAIN BARREL

There are many advantages to using rainwater to water your plants. It doesn't have the additives tap water does and it tends to be less acidic, so it is gentler on plants. It is also richer in nitrogen, which explains why rain lilies *(Zephyranthes)* bloom more profusely when watered with rainwater.

Rain barrels provide an easy way to collect this valuable resource from any roof. For every 1,000 square feet of roof and inch of rain, you will get 600 gallons of water. Rain barrels can be made out of oak, plastic, or ceramic. Simply run the downspout from your gutters into the top of the barrel and use water as needed.

Gardeners love to talk about the weather. In fact, many keep journals of the weather in their area and how much rain they have received from year to year. This easy-to-make rain gauge can also measure water from overhead sprinklers to make sure the garden is adequately irrigated when rainfall is scarce. However, the collection jar must be at least 1 foot off the ground to ensure that no water splashes into the gauge, yet low enough to minimize the effects of wind on measurements. In addition, it should be located away from structures or trees and be set level (with a carpenter's level) to be perfectly calibrated.

An accurate rain gauge requires a cylindrical "collector" with an opening at least 3 inches wide. Cylindrical floral vases work perfectly for this. For this project, four dowels set into the top of a post hold the collecting jar in place and allow it to be removed and emptied easily.

1. Mark positions for dowels on top of post by centering jar or vase on top of post: hold a dowel perpendicular to the edge of jar at each corner and trace the dowel with a pencil. Mark all 4 dowel locations.

2. Using ⅜" brad point bit, drill out holes for all 4 dowels, each about 2" deep and perpendicular to the surface of post.

3. Clean out sawdust from holes, dab dowels with wood glue, and insert them in holes.

4. Thoroughly clean glass jar or vase. Roughen back surface of the stainless steel ruler with steel wool or sandpaper, to increase surface adhesion of epoxy. In a well-ventilated area, mix epoxy following manufacturer's instructions and apply to back side of ruler. Affix ruler to wall of cylinder so that the zero point is lined up with bottom of cylinder and the ruler runs straight up the side of cylinder, perpendicular to cylinder's base.

5. Set 4x4 cedar post into ground, to a depth of at least 1 foot, selecting a site matching the instructions above and using a level to ensure that its top is level. After epoxy dries, place jar on top of post between the dowels. Wait for rain.

MATERIALS

One 4"×4"×3' cedar post
4 pieces of ⅜" hardwood
    doweling, 9½" long
Exterior wood glue
Glass jar or vase, 9" tall
    and 3" in diameter
6" stainless steel ruler
5-minute outdoor epoxy
Steel wool or coarse
    sandpaper

TOOLS

Miter saw with finish blade
Drill
⅜" brad point drill bit
Tape measure
Level
Pencil

FAUCET HANDLE COATRACK

MATERIALS

One 1"x6"x3' red cedar board

One 2"×4"×1' red cedar board
    or scrap cedar

Vintage faucet and/or valve
    handles

Brass screws, about 1½" long
    (see Note)

2" brass screws (2)
    for hanging

Brass washers (see Note)

Exterior wood glue

Wood finish (optional)

TOOLS

Pencil

Tape measure

Flathead screwdriver

Drill

Drill bit sized to brass screws

Table saw

Miter saw

Palm sander

Fine-grade sandpaper

NOTE

The heads of your screws and
    the washers need to cover
    the center holes of the
    faucet handles, so match
    the sizes appropriately.

Everyone has a coatrack *inside* the house, but why not have one on a covered porch or in the garage so that you don't have to take your work boots off to go inside for a coat when the weather takes a turn? It's also a handy place to store hats, convenient when you're working outside and a cloudy day turns into a sunny one. This whimsical rack, made from new or vintage faucets, is perfect for rain slickers, hats, and your favorite work shirt.

1. Using a miter saw, cut the 1×6 cedar board to a desired length based on the number and size of handles used. In our case, we cut the 1×6 to 32" for 5 handles. Use palm sander to bevel the edges of the face.

2. Using table or miter saw, rip down 2×4 or any scrap cedar available into as many 1"×1"×1" blocks as there are faucet handles.

3. With the 1×6 lying flat, position the blocks on the 1×6 so they are spaced evenly apart, or in a pattern to your liking. Glue these blocks into position and let dry. Once the glue has cured, drill a pilot hole through the center of each of the 1"×1" blocks. Apply wood finish, if desired.

4. Using brass screw and washers, screw each handle to a block, carefully hand-tightening screws. Brass is a soft metal and too much pressure may snap the screw or strip the screw head. Drill additional holes 1 inch in from the top corners to hang the rack. Use the same style brass screws (of a longer length) and washers to affix to the wall. Set the washers over screw holes to prevent damage to cedar, which is soft.

MATERIALS

Submersible fountain pump
  with adjustable flow and 6"
  piece of ½" flexible tubing
  (see Notes)
Half a whiskey barrel or a
  large glazed ceramic pot
  (see Notes)
1 rubber stopper (optional)
One 2'3" piece of 1"-diameter
  bamboo pole
One 6" piece of ½"-diameter
  bamboo pole
Clear waterproof caulk
Bricks (enough to hold
  fountain pump and pots in
  place)
2 terra-cotta or glazed pots
  (optional)
Glass mulch or decorative
  stones (optional)

TOOLS

⅝" ship auger bit (typically
  about 1' to 1'3" of drilling
  length)
Bit the diameter of
  smaller bambool pole,
  approximately ½"
Paddle bit that matches
  exterior diameter of the
  2'3" bamboo piece (see
  Notes)
¼" drill bit or a rat-tail file
Miter saw or handsaw
Utility knife

The sound of running water is soothing to the mind and the spirit. Bamboo fountains have always been placed outside Japanese shrines for worshippers to wash their hands before entering. A fountain in front of the house can help mask the sound of a noisy street, and makes a wonderful addition to any garden.

1. With a miter saw or handsaw, cut the 1"-diameter bamboo pole down to 27" to 30". The pole should be cut so that a node is close to one end. This end will become the top. The node will block the water from flowing out the top of the fountain. The other 2 nodes should be reachable from the bottom end of the bamboo with the ship auger bit. Drill out these 2 nodes with the ship auger bit.

2. Cut ½"-diameter bamboo pole to a 6" length. If there is any pulp inside the piece, use a ¼" drill bit or rat-tail file to remove the pulp so that water flow is not restricted.

3. Cut one end of the 6" piece at a 45-degree angle for the waterspout.

4. With bit the diameter of 6" bamboo, drill a hole into the side of the 1"-diameter pole that matches the outside diameter of the 6" piece of bamboo. The hole should be centered on the 1"-diameter bamboo and drilled perpendicular to the length of the 1" bamboo pole.

5. Slip the flat end of the 6" piece of bamboo into the hole. Use clear caulking to seal the hole. Set aside and allow to dry, following manufacturer's instructions.

6. Slip tubing into the bottom of the 1" bamboo pole as far as it will go.

7. Cut flexible tubing off with a utility knife, leaving ¼" protruding from the end of the bamboo pole. Slip the pump's adapter into the end of the tubing to join pole to pump.

8. Set the pole and pump into barrel or large ceramic pot (see Notes) and place bricks or gravel around the pump to hold it in place.

9. If you like, set empty terra-cotta or glazed pots in the bottom of container to serve as holders for potted water plants. This will make it easer to swap plants in and out of fountain as needed.

10. Cover the bottom of the container with bricks to raise the floor. Use glass mulch or decorative stones to cover the bricks, if desired.

11. Fill with water. Remember to set fountain in place first, as it will be difficult once filled with water. Oak barrels may leak when first filled, but eventually staves will swell and become watertight.

12. Plug the fountain into a GFCI (ground fault circuit interrupter) outlet. Adjust pump to create desired flow.

NOTES

Select a pump that will power a fountain with a maximum height of 3'6".

If you use a large glazed ceramic pot, choose one without a drainage hole, or plug the hole with a rubber stopper or caulk it closed.

Some plants, such as water lilies, prefer to grow in calm water, while others, such as water irises, grow well in moving water. Be careful to choose plants that will not mind the movement a fountain creates.

Bamboo is a natural material and its diameter varies. The paddle bit should have a diameter about ⅜" less than the diameter of the bamboo.

BULBS

From onions and garlic to tulips and daffodils, bulbs are really modified underground shoots that store food and provide us with savory meals and beautiful flowers. And, as any gardener will tell you at bulb-planting time in the fall, their tunic-covered bulbs offer much more than that—they contain the promise of another spring.

MATERIALS

Container, 10 to 14 inches
    deep
Soilless potting medium
Turkey grit or gravel
A variety of bulbs for forcing,
    such as alliums, hyacinths,
    Muscari (grape hyacinth),
    fritillaria, crocuses, tulips,
    snowdrops, narcissus, and
    daffodils
Mulch, such as buckwheat
    hulls or cocoa shells

Gardeners often have the best intentions when ordering fall bulbs for planting, but occasionally all the bulbs don't make it into the ground (this is the horticultural equivalent of an overloaded plate at a picnic). Though these bulbs can be potted up and forced for indoor use, they can also be potted up in a container. Given a chill-down period (for some climates this can be done outdoors, for others in an unheated garage or cellar, and for snowbirds in warm climates the containers can be chilled in an old refrigerator), in spring these containers can be set by the door to share their delightful flowers. By layering them, you can extend the bloom cycle by up to a month. Once the flowers have gone by, replant the planter with annuals and tender perennials for the summer.

When selecting bulbs for forcing, consult catalogs or store displays to get bulbs that force well. Some varieties and genera force more easily than others.

• *Photograph on page 194*

1. Combine potting mix with grit or gravel—about 3 parts soilless mix to 1 part gravel. This will ensure that the bulbs have the drainage they prefer.

2. Lay out bulbs to be planted. They can be planted in layers in the pot to maximize container's bloom period. As a general rule, smaller bulbs should be planted above larger bulbs in containers as if making a layered salad, with potting mix in between to allow the roots to develop. Characteristics such as bloom period, color, height, and fragrance should be considered. Early-flowering hyacinths offer heady fragrance in containers along walkways and at entrances, and daffodils and tulips provide flowers after hyacinths bloom. Small bulbs around the edges of the container will provide additional color and blooms.

3. Begin by adding 2-inch layer of potting mix to container and then plant a layer of tall-growing bulbs, such as tulips or daffodils, at a depth of 6 to 8 inches. Cover with 3 inches of potting mix, add a layer of low-growing bulbs such as hyacinths or *Muscari,* and cover with another another layer of soil. Each layer can contain groupings of different bulbs, but the final layer of soil should cover all bulbs by 3 inches. Add a 1" layer of mulch on top. Water in well.

4. Store in a cool, dark place with steady temperatures below 50 degrees but above freezing, and water occasionally if planting seems to dry out. After about 15 weeks (roughly the chilling period for plants to set roots), the container can be moved outside and exposed to some light to encourage leaf development. Bulbs in containers are more susceptible to extremes of heat or cold than those in the ground. If weather is subject to heavy freezes, move small containers to a sheltered area or an unheated garage or shed (with windows for light) to protect them from freezing. In warmer areas, bulbs may be placed in a refrigerator, although being stored with any fruit that gives off ethylene gas, such as apples, will inhibit bulb growth. Large containers can be set into bales of hay. In warm climates, make sure containers stay cool enough and position out of direct sunlight during cool-down period.

Though many Americans understand the pleasure of growing their own tomatoes and fresh vegetables, fewer people go a step further and grow their own garlic, shallots, and onions. However, homegrown garlic, onions, and shallots have a freshness and sweetness that are hard to replicate with store-bought varieties. By growing, and then curing, a variety of edible alliums, the home gardener will be provided with the delightful flavor of these beloved bulbs all year long.

Onion and shallot sets can be planted out in early spring as soon as the ground can be worked, or they can be started indoors from seed. Plant in groups of three or four if garden space is at a premium. As onions are biennial, they may bolt and set seed if conditions are too hot or dry, but keeping them well watered and monitoring planting time can help to prevent this.

Garlic is traditionally planted in the fall in the North and in the spring or fall in warmer climates. To plant garlic, set out a clove from a bulb, point side up. Large cloves are best for growing to bulbs, but the small ones can also be planted and enjoyed as garlic scallions in the early spring. There are two groups of garlic: soft-neck and stiff-neck, or hard-neck. Stiff-neck tends to be larger and is easier to peel. Stiff-neck garlic will need to have its flower stalk broken off midseason, but this is edible as well. Soft-neck is a great garlic for storage and is the one typically used in braiding.

HARVESTING

When onion and garlic foliage starts to turn yellow or brown and falls over, the bulbs are ready to harvest. In most areas this happens between mid and late summer. Beyond this time the bulbs will toughen and cease increasing in size. Push over any greens that have not fallen over naturally and harvest onions within two weeks of foliage browning. When 30 to 50 percent of garlic foliage has turned brown and fallen over, it too is ready to harvest.

CURING

Garlic and onions must be cured to prevent mold or rot from developing. To do this, simply separate the bulbs and set them on a screen in a shaded area. Alternatively, tie them and hang them in clusters from the rafters. They will cure in about two weeks and can then be braided. If they are not to be braided, they should be topped and tailed.

TOPPING AND TAILING

After onions and garlic have cured, cut their tops and roots off (known as topping and tailing). Cut off the dried greens about 1 to 2 inches above the bulb. Using scissors, trim back the whiskers of the root as closely as possible without damaging bulb. Store in a cool, dry place in mesh bags or open baskets for good air circulation. Onions and garlic can last up to 6 months if stored in the right conditions. They will begin to sprout if they are in too warm an environment.

BRAIDING

When topping and tailing onions and garlic for braiding, leave stalks on, merely tailing the bulb with scissors. Lay the first bulb of onion or garlic on a worktable. Point its roots toward the opposite end of the table. Lay the second bulb on top of the first bulb, with its stalks pointing out at a 45-degree angle to the right, then a third on top of the second, with its stalks pointing out at a 45-degree angle to the left. Hold the pile in place at the crossing of the stalks. Take the first stalk and wrap it over the top, then back under the second and third stalks where they cross, until the first stalk is pointing back in its original direction. This will prevent the bottom of braid from unraveling.

Continue laying down additional bulbs—after each wrap, as above, and placed in the center of the braid—and braiding stalks as though braiding hair. When desired length is reached, simply braid remaining stalks and tie off at top. Hang in a cool, dry place and harvest as needed, from the top of the braid down, by cutting off individual bulbs.

ONION BASKET PLANTER
Planting in tiers makes a wonderful waterfall effect and, with the conversion of an old onion basket from the kitchen into a sphagnum-moss-lined planter, this effect can be created with relative ease. A drought-tolerant plant reduces the chances of these plants drying out, but a collection of small ferns hanging in a shady nook is also lovely.

Dahlias are great additions to any flower border. Because they are so prolific, they're also ideal for cutting. Although perennial in some parts of the country, they are not hardy in colder areas. The tubers can be planted in spring after the danger of frost is past and the soil begins to warm up. Some gardeners get a head start by potting tubers up and starting them indoors, and many gardeners save their favorite varieties (there are more than 20,000 cultivars) by digging up the tubers once the stems of the plants have been blackened by frost. The tubers simply need to be washed clean of all soil and the stem cut off, leaving only about 2 inches behind. Then they can be stored in boxes of sand, vermiculite, or cedar mulch in a cool, dark place until the next spring. At that point, tubers are divided (a bit of stem is left with each tuber) and then replanted. To keep cultivars separate and marked, use the mesh bags in which onions or fall-planted bulbs arrive, adding a tag to the drawstring to label each variety.

Cannas and other nonhardy bulbs can be pulled and stored in the same manner.

Onionskins have been used throughout history as a natural dye for fabrics and yarns because of their rich golds and soft yellow-greens. In the spring, onionskins are sometimes collected for dyeing Easter eggs as well.

The marbled patterns on these eggs are so beautiful that you may wish to keep them on display permanently. If stored in a dry place, the eggs will dry out over time and can be kept indefinitely—surprisingly, they do not smell of rotten eggs. A bowl of them can make a wonderful centerpiece, but why not set out a plate of freshly cooked eggs as part of a casual brunch? The leftover peeled onions can be used to make onion marmalade to go with brunch.

MATERIALS AND TOOLS

1 dozen white eggs

2 cups onionskins, both red and yellow

Cotton rags or cheesecloth

Rubber bands

Saucepan

1. Soak onionskins in a bowl of cool water till soft.

2. Cut rags or cheesecloth into pieces (1 for each egg) approximately 8 inches square.

3. Wet surface of egg and wrap with softened onionskins as for papier-mâché, laying several layers of skin over each egg. Wet a piece of cloth and wrap around onionskin-covered egg, making sure egg is held snugly in cloth. Use rubber band to hold cloth in place. Repeat with remaining eggs.

4. Set eggs in a saucepan of water. Bring water to a rolling boil and cook eggs until hard-boiled (5 to 7 minutes after water begins boiling).

5. Drain hot water from pan and fill with cool water. When eggs are cool enough to handle comfortably, remove from water and gently take off cloth pouches and onionskins. Rinse eggs with cool water and serve.

HARVEST

From picking apples—the last fruit of the season for many of us—to carving pumpkins, the fall harvest is prized for its bounty of late season produce. It also holds a special place in our hearts as we reflect on the passing growing season and begin to prepare for the next spring. And what is more captivating than the beauty of a living fence of apples, ready for harvest.

6 apple or pear trees of
  ½" to ¾" caliper trunks,
  preferably grown on dwarf
  or semi-dwarf stock

TOOLS

Graph paper
Pencil
Plastic tape
Shovel
Twine
Pruning shears

Espaliers are a time-honored way to grow apples and create a living fence out of trees. A Belgian fence is a style of espalier in which limbs are trained into a lattice-like pattern. It is a space-saving device imported from Europe, where it has been popular since at least the eighteenth century. Espaliers are constructed for their ease of harvest and increased fruit production. Many woody plants can be trained in this manner, but apple and pear trees are the classic plants for this pattern. Varieties of the same fruit can be used, such as Roxbury Russets and Gala apples or even a mix of apples and pears. Select young trees or whips, with ½" to ¾" caliper trunks and set them against wire or hog wire attached to a frame, to support them while training them into place.

Belgian fences can be trained against a range of surfaces, from a brick wall and chainlink fence to a section of hog wire set between two cedar posts and held in a dadoed groove with screws (as in illustration) or, as in our friend Peter Wooster's garden, through a series of cedar posts with wire strung across at regular intervals (see page 204).

The best time to start an espalier is several weeks before the tree breaks dormancy in late winter or early spring, because the plant will have a more vigorous response to the pruning cuts made after planting. The technique can also be done in cooler fall temperatures. A full-fledged fence can be developed in three to four seasons.

This project is for a 6-foot-long fence, but you can increase the length to as much as 40 feet. Use the fence in the center of a long hedge as a window into an adjoining area of the garden. • *Photograph on page 204*

1. Select a site for the Belgian fence where the trees will receive a full day's sun and amend soil as needed. Create a support for the trees to be trained against. Trees can also be trained on an already existing fence, although unless it is chain link, attach turnbuckles, to extend 8" out from fence to provide air circulation for the trees, and guy wires.

2. Draw out design on graph paper. The traditional design of the Belgian fence involves trees planted 18 inches on center (the distance from one tree's trunk to the adjacent trunk), with a pattern of branches angling off at 45 degrees from the base of the trunks about 16" from the ground. These branches will be created by pruning and getting dormant buds to break, so don't worry if tree does not branch that low. The trees at each end of the fence will have one branch angled at 45 degrees toward the rest of the Belgian fence, with the other branch trained perpendicular to the ground. The pattern should resemble an argyle sweater, with lines forming diamonds.

3. Using plastic tape, set out design on the structure you have chosen, starting with first tree 1' in from end of structure and ending 1' before other end with final tree. Set trees in place and plant them, ideally setting in so dormant buds are at point where tape pattern divides into first branch pattern for each tree. Water in plants.

4. Look at the buds on the tree to decide where to cut. Dormant buds look like small, slightly raised breaks in the tree's bark. Look for outward-facing buds that are already pointing in the right direction at the spot or slightly above where pattern on fence angles off. Cut each tree with sharp pruning shears above the chosen buds. This will get the tree to restart or branch at the desired place. Never cut below the first 6" of the main stem, as apples and pears are grafted onto rootstock and the tree won't come true to its variety if cut below the graft.

5. Using twine, tie the main stem to the support fence. In about 3 to 4 weeks, buds will grow on. Point the new stems in the desired direction of pattern and tie them on the support when they are about 6" long. The end pieces will have one piece going up at 90 degrees and the other stem at 45 degrees, and the interior trees will have each branch trained up at 45 degrees in each direction. Continue to tie in stems as they grow on, to train them along tape lines.

6. The Belgian fence will be mature in 3 years or so. During that time, cut back undesired shoots that come off the main pattern to the bud nearest the branch to which it is attached. Creating these spurs will also encourage fruiting.

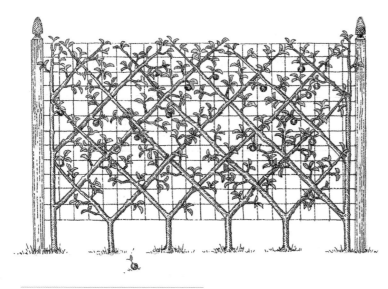

A simple support can be made using cedar posts and agricultural fencing

Tripod orchard ladders are the primary tools used in harvesting apples and other tree fruits. The narrowing tapered form allows the ladder to fit between the branches of the tree when picking fruit, and the tripod makes it stable, less prone to tipping or becoming unbalanced. Like many workaday objects, the beauty of these orchard ladders also makes them a wonderful inspiration for a plant stand (the one pictured was built with small begonias and African violets in mind but can also display curios and a miniature fern or two). Since the ladder is meant to last for years to come, splurging on oak or elm will ensure its strength, and many orchard ladders were traditionally made of these long-lasting hardwoods.

1. Use miter saw to cut a 49½" length from both 1"×6" boards. Use table saw to rip down the lengths to 4½" wide. Set aside remaining ⅞" pieces to be used as cross braces.

2. Set miter saw blade to 20 degrees (to the right) and to a 4-degree bevel. To create left rail, first lay one 4½" board flat and cut right end. Then slide board to the right of the blade and trim left end so that final length is 47".

3. Set miter saw blade to 20 degrees to the left (retaining 4-degree bevel). Repeat steps above in step 2 to create right rail.

4. Install ¾" dado blade on table saw. Set blade to height of ⅜" and to a bevel of 4 degrees.

5. Create 4 slots on the inside of each rail, for the steps of ladder. Starting 3" from bottom of rail, cut a ¾" dado slot parallel to the cut ends. Position the cut so the deeper side of slot (resulting from the bevel) is at top of slot. Use a piece of scrap wood on back side of cut to prevent blowout of rail material. Dado each of 3 remaining slots 10" up from top of previous slot.

6. Use remaining 1"×6" stock for steps. Set miter saw to 4 degrees in order to bevel both sides of each step. Cut steps to lengths (measured on longest edge): 23", 20½", 18", and 15⅝".

7. Cut top step (or cap) to 14½"×5³⁄₁₆".

8. Install finish blade on table saw and set blade to 20 degrees. Bevel-cut the long sides of each step to produce steps 4¾" wide. When installed, beveled edges will sit flush with angle of rails.

[CONTINUED]

MATERIALS

One 1"×6"×8' oak board
One 1"×6"×10' oak board
One 1"×2"×6' oak board
1¼" and 1" wood screws
Wood glue
2' of ⅜" wood doweling
Wood finish

TOOLS

Table saw
Miter saw with finish blade
¾" dado blade
Drill
Countersink drill bit
Bit for drilling pilot holes
Flush saw
Tape measure
Framing square
Pencil
Hand or palm sander
Fine-grade sandpaper

9. Dry-fit steps into slots on rails and drill 2 pilot holes into ends of each step through rails. Countersink each hole. Disassemble, glue, and secure steps with 1¼" wood screws.

10. Center cap and attach with glue and 1¼" wood screws.

11. Cut tripod brace to size using 1"×2" stock. Brace length should be ¾"×1½"×44⅜" with 10-degree angles at either end.

12. Using miter saw, create 1"×3" cleat with a 10-degree bevel lengthwise and attach to the underside of cap. Position cleat 1" in from back edge of cap and center between the ends. Fasten with two 1¼" wood screws.

13. Using miter saw, with excess material from initial cuts, create two 20¾"×⅞"×¾" cross braces connecting tripod leg to the underside of second step. Set miter saw blade to 24 degrees (to the right). Install a fence on the miter saw to position the brace material perpendicular to the saw's fixed fence (i.e., parallel to the blade) and cut the end of each brace at a 24-degree angle. Remove the second fence so the braces can be positioned against the saw's fixed fence (i.e., perpendicular to the blade) and set the blade to a 10-degree bevel (while retaining the 24-degree angle). Cut other end of left brace to a length of 20¾". Reposition the blade 24 degrees to the left with 10-degree bevel and cut other end of right brace.

14. Position tripod leg against cleat on underside of cap, predrill, countersink, and secure with 1" screws. Attach cross braces and secure with 1" screws through predrilled and countersunk holes.

15. Cover all screws except 2 with ⅜" dowel, attaching tripod leg to cleat and braces to second step. Leave these accessible so tripod leg can be removed. Glue dowels and cut them flush.

16. After glue dries, sand ladder and apply finish.

WEED BASKET
A simple wooden basket hanging on a gate or a fence near the garden
prevents you from leaving little piles of weeds throughout the garden
to be picked up later (or, sometimes, forgotten). It can be hung from
an S-hook or a simple nail, then whisked off to the compost pile to be
emptied and rehung for the next round of weeds.

MATERIALS

Wooden bushel basket, with woven bottom 12" inches or larger in diameter

Clamp light, with shade and clamp removed

2 plywood disks (available at craft stores), 3 inches in diameter

One $\frac{1}{8}$ IP threaded nipple $1\frac{1}{2}$" long (see Note)

Two $\frac{1}{8}$ IP brass locknuts

Twine

Lamp hanging hoop and chain (optional)

TOOLS

Pliers

Drill

$\frac{1}{2}$" drill bit

Craft scissors

NOTE

The threaded nipple and locknuts are available in the lighting section of the hardware store.

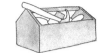 There is something inherently nostalgic about wooden bushel baskets. They evoke memories of a childhood trip to pick apples in the country or of a neighbor dropping off a bushel of apricots, and they epitomize the simple life.

The wood strips these baskets are made from are thin enough to let a warm glow of light pass through, which makes them wonderful lantern shades for covered outdoor spaces. We are not alone in our love of these simple forms: when Frank Gehry designed a collection of bentwood furniture for the esteemed furniture-maker Knoll, he claimed that these simple bushel baskets were his inspiration.

You can build the light fixture yourself, but everyday clamp lights from big box stores are UL rated and inexpensive, providing a perfect light source if you're nervous about doing your own electrical work. If this light is to be hardwired to an outlet, it is best to use supplies from a lamp shop or the lighting section of the hardware store.

1. Use pliers to carefully remove the staples from the center bottom of the bushel basket. Then, using an old pair of craft scissors (cutting may dull blades), cut out a 2"×2" square from the center of each wood layer on the bottom of the basket.

2. Drill a $\frac{1}{2}$-inch hole in the center of the 2 plywood disks. Set aside.

3. Take clamp light and unscrew socket to access wires inside: set aside outer socket casing. Unscrew wire ends from inner socket and untie them. Set inner part of socket aside. Slide cord out of the hole in base of socket. Screw threaded nipple into hole at base of socket.

4. Insert threaded nipple through one of the plywood disks. Screw a locknut onto threaded nipple and tighten it against the disk.

5. Insert threaded nipple through hole in bottom of basket, then through second disk. Screw another nut onto threaded nipple and loosely tighten. Center disk on bottom of basket.

6. Cut a piece of twine twice the desired length of final hanging height of lamp. Fold in half and slide center point under disk on bottom of lamp and wrap it once around threaded nipple. Adjust twine so it comes out beneath the disk on opposite sides. Tie a knot in twine centered over threaded nipple. The apple basket will hang from this twine. Alternatively, the nipple can be attached to a lamp-hanging hoop and chain can be added.

7. Reattach electrical cord by sliding it through center of threaded nipple from outside to inside of basket. Retie split ends of wire as they were when socket was first opened. Wrap wire ends around screws onto either side of inner socket and tighten. Push wire back through threaded nipple until casing is realigned with socket and switch. Screw on remaining piece of the outer socket casing.

8. Hang the apple basket lantern from twine. To avoid stressing electrical cord, make sure lamp's weight is supported by twine or chain rather than by the cord.

Strings of lights hanging outdoors evoke wonderful memories for all of us—perhaps a trip to Italy or a summer night on a friend's terrace. By simply creating copper mesh shades for inexpensive stringed lights, you can have that same magical glow cast upon any porch or terrace. The copper will take on a patina over time that only enriches the experience.

1. Using metal shears or utility scissors, cut one 4"×10" rectangle of metal mesh for every lightbulb on the strand.

2. Carefully fold each side of copper mesh rectangle over ¼", then fold each edge over again another ¼". Repeat with remaining rectangles.

3. Starting with first bulb on strand, take finished mesh rectangle and fold it around bulb so that it forms a cone. The point of the cone should be set above individual lightbulb socket and the open end should hang over top of bulb. When cone is in place, the short side of mesh rectangle should be flush with opposite edge of long side. Using an awl or knitting needle, poke a hole through both layers of mesh where corner of short end of rectangle meets the opening of cone.

4. Insert paper fastener into hole and splay prongs on back so they hold cone in place. Repeat with remaining bulbs.

MATERIALS

Copper or brass mesh fabric (available at craft stores)

Metal shears or utility scissors

Paper fasteners (the old-fashioned brass variety)

String of 1½-inch lights with 5-watt bulbs (if your lights are larger or smaller, you may need to adjust the size of your mesh pieces in step 1)

Awl or knitting needle

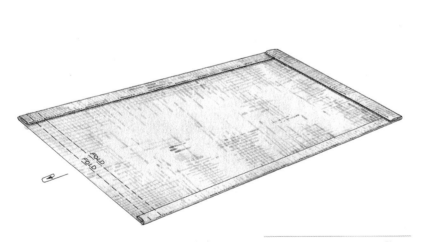

Step 2

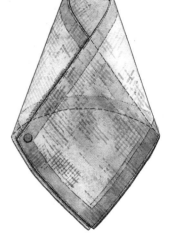

Step 4

MATERIALS AND TOOLS

1 dry, clean gourd (see Note)

Drill

2½" bit

Boiling water and large bowl
(optional)

Double-sided gourd-cleaning
tool (available online) or
knife and spoon

Rotary tool such as a Dremel

Rotary tool drill bits in varying
sizes, such as ¹⁄₁₆" and ³⁄₃₂"

Grinding bit for carving
or sanding rough edges
(optional)

Wood glue (optional)

Wooden low-wattage light
base for 2½" hole

Pencil

NOTE

If you are working with a gourd
that is dry but not yet clean,
wash and scrub the gourd
in a mild solution of bleach
and water to remove any
black mold on the surface.

Gourds have been cultivated for thousands of years for use as bowls, vessels, and musical instruments. With a simple low-wattage light fixture and a rotary tool, they can be transformed into charming lights.

1. With 2½" drill bit, drill a hole centered on the bottom of the gourd.

2. If the seeds and flesh are a solid ball inside gourd, break up with a knife or a gourd-cleaning tool. Pull out dried seeds and flesh. If majority of seeds and flesh are attached to walls of gourd, carefully fill with boiling water and prop it, bottom side up, in a large bowl so flesh can soften, for about ½ hour. When flesh has softened, use knife and spoon or gourd tool to scrape it out.

3. Draw your drilling pattern on gourd with pencil.

4. Begin drilling pattern with rotary tool and desired bits to create perforations, following pattern penciled on gourd.

5. To create larger round holes, use a larger drill bit. For freeform holes, use the ¹⁄₁₆" bit to drill holes very close together around the shape you want to cut out. With the rotary tool on, drag bit from point to point as if connecting the dots to cut out the shape. Use a grinding bit, if desired, to clean up any rough edges.

6. When you have finished drilling your pattern, set light base in hole in bottom of gourd. Either press the base in place or glue it in place. Be aware that gluing it in place may complicate matters when it is time to change the bulb.

DRILLING SQUASH
With a drill and an array of bits, you can make interesting luminaria in minutes out of a variety of heirloom squash. The end result should garner as much admiration as an intricately carved pumpkin.

There are so many varieties of heirloom pumpkins and squash worth growing. Provided they are isolated from other varieties, their seeds can be easily saved. Simply remove seeds from pumpkins (if the pumpkins are picked fully ripened and cured afterward, the seed will be its most viable), rinse clean of all pulpy matter, and set aside on paper plates in a cool, dry place out of direct sunlight. Once seeds make a strong snapping noise when broken in half, store in manila envelopes in a covered jar with a packet of silica gel in the refrigerator.

To cure pumpkins and squash after picking, set them in a cool, dry place up off the ground with good air circulation for three weeks. Curing them in this manner will allow them to keep longer, so that they can be used through much of the fall and winter.

Sugar pumpkins are wonderful for cooking, as are many other varieties of squash. This toothsome gratin is a perfect accompaniment to grilled meats but easily makes a hearty lunch or light supper on its own.

1. Preheat an oven or a grill to 375 degrees F. In a small mixing bowl, combine salt, pepper, and flour. Set aside.

2. Butter a deep baking dish or cast-iron skillet. Begin to layer the vegetables, starting with onion. Follow with a layer of pumpkin, then sprinkle with the seasoned flour. Next, add a layer of cauliflower, then a sprinkling of Fontina cheese. Continue layering, alternating the vegetables, seasoned flour, and Fontina, making sure that your top layer is pumpkin.

3. Pour the half-and-half over the top and place on the grill or in the oven. If cooking on grill, place baking dish over indirect heat. While the gratin bakes, combine ingredients for topping and mix thoroughly.

4. After about 30 minutes, sprinkle gratin with bread crumb topping and bake for an additional 45 minutes. Let gratin settle for 10 minutes or more before serving.

SERVES 6 TO 8 AS A LIGHT LUNCH OR SIDE DISH

1½ teaspoons salt
1½ teaspoons pepper
2 tablespoons all-purpose flour
Butter
1 medium purple onion, thinly sliced
1 sugar pumpkin, peeled, seeded, and sliced into ¼-inch-thick wedges
1 medium head cauliflower, sliced down the center into ¼-inch-thick pieces
½ cup finely diced Fontina cheese
1½ cups half-and-half

BREAD CRUMB TOPPING
1 cup panko (Japanese-style) bread crumbs
1 tablespoon melted butter
¾ cup grated Parmesan
3 tablespoons lightly toasted pine nuts

TREES

From the elm-lined streets that once spanned the nation and the redwood forests of Northern California to the acres of sugar maples of the Northeast and the palms overhanging Florida beaches, trees provide us with shade, nuts, maple sugar, and wood. They also inspire an awe for the sheer power of the plant kingdom. From the aspirin first derived from a chemical produced by willow trees to the leaves dropped each fall for addition to our compost bins, trees help care for the world around us. Our planting of young saplings is a testament to our love of these majestic plants.

Gardeners always try to consider the right plant for the right place. This adage holds truer for trees and shrubs than it does for perennials and annuals. It is important to take time when siting a tree to ensure that the decision takes into account the long term as well as the tree's next few seasons. One of the simplest pieces of advice is to set the tree on the spot where it is to be planted and wait a few days before planting it (watering it as needed in the interim). This will provide time to consider the location and see it from all angles, including the kitchen window. • *Photograph on page 222*

Here are some other factors to consider:

- Carefully plot out the areas where you are going to plant a tree and think about how the tree will grow into the space.

- Determine where the tree will cast its shade at different times of the day and year. Set a tall bamboo stake into the ground and watch where its shadow falls during the day. The tree will cast its shadow in the same direction as the stake. You can then tell whether it will provide shade on the terrace in the afternoon or cut out the sun that a flower border depends on. Consider as well the changing position of the sun, not only through the day but over the course of the seasons—for instance, it's lower in the sky during the winter, which will affect shadows as well.

- You'll have to dodge or mow around a tree in the middle of the lawn. It also may shade out the grass underneath it.

- Consider the tree's ultimate size in planting it. Will it block a favorite view or cover an unsightly one? Is it too near the house and will it create shade that will cause mildew and mold to grow on the house's siding? Will its roots affect storm drains or the house's foundation?

- How quickly will it grow? Will it outgrow the area it was selected to cover?

- Will it create a windbreak from cold winter winds? Traditionally, evergreens are often grown as winter windbreaks, while deciduous shade trees are sited to give us respite from summer sun while letting in much-desired winter light.

- Do you want a single-stemmed or multiple-stemmed tree? Multistemmed trees can add visual interest and naturalistic style to the landscape.

- Consider whether you want to plant it straight or leaning at an angle. For centuries, Japanese gardeners have planted trees leaning at an angle to create the illusion of age.

- Do you want it to offer a sense of privacy or screening?

Willow has been used for medicinal purposes for centuries—in fact, one of its components was used first in making aspirin. Willow also has other chemicals that help plants to root. Though willow roots so easily that all you need to do is stick cuttings of it in moist soil, a water made from boiling willow branches will help to root cuttings of other plants, from roses and lilacs to salvias and azaleas.

To make willow water, gather about 2 cups of pencil-thin willow branches and cut to 1 to 3-inch lengths. Steep twigs in ½ gallon of boiling water overnight.

Cuttings of plants to be propagated can be steeped in willow water before setting out. Alternatively, soil can be watered with the willow water to promote root growth. Two applications should be sufficient. Some cuttings, such as coleus, will root directly in a jar of willow water. Make a fresh batch of willow water for each use.

Refrigerated liquid kept in a jar with a tight-fitting lid will remain effective up to 2 months.

SCULPTURAL WILLOW LAMP

MATERIALS

Scrap ¾" plywood (enough for 15" circle)

Cylinder-style light fixture, preferably with a switch on its cord

40 to 60 curly willow branches, 4' to 5' long (available through floral suppliers)

¾" long wood screws

Spray paint (optional)

Wood glue

TOOLS

Jigsaw

Fine-grade sandpaper

Drill

Drill bit matched to diameter of larger willow branches

Mat knife

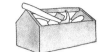

The sculptural form of a backlit tree, with its branches glowing in the late-afternoon sun, is a beautiful sight to behold. Using these curly willow branches to encircle a simple store-bought light base allows you to bring the same effect indoors, at the ready to cast its magical glow with the flick of a switch.

1. Cut a 15-inch circle out of plywood with a jigsaw.

2. Lightly sand around the edges of the circle.

3. Drill holes all the way around the outer edge of the circle, about ⅜ inch apart and ⅜ inch in from outer edge of circle.

4. If desired, spray-paint the circle and let it dry.

5. Fasten the light fixture to the center of the circle. Fixtures vary, so check the bottom of the fixture and adjust attachment method as needed. Most can be attached with simple screws into the base, but be sure not to allow screws to extend beyond the bottom of the base.

6. Using mat knife, trim the ends of the twigs so that they are flat on the bottom, and whittle any sides necessary if they are too large to fit snugly in the holes around the circle.

7. Place a dab of wood glue in first hole, set in twig, and hold in place so that twig is curving toward center of circle. Repeat process with remaining holes and twigs, until there are only 4 or 5 unfilled holes adjacent to one another.

8. Do not glue the last few twigs in place; simply set them in holes, making sure they sit in firmly, so they can be removed when lightbulb needs replacing. If you like, remaining twigs may be interwoven across the top of branches in a basket-weave pattern to strengthen structure, but this is not necessary and will make sculptural quality of the upright twigs less apparent.

It is always exciting to rethink an ordinary component of the backyard landscape and turn it into something visually appealing. A serpentine woodpile can hide unsightly problems—for instance, a raised septic system or the work area at the back of your yard—while providing an attractive and functional way to store firewood. It can also make an interesting temporary fence or wall at the back end of your property.

1. With a garden hose serving as a guideline for the front edge of the woodpile, lay out the design you want. Keep in mind that if its curves are too sharp, it will be harder to stack the wood and the design will be less elegant.

2. Begin arranging the wood along the back side of the garden hose. The bottommost layer of the woodpile may be subject to rot if it is not laid on a surface that drains or dries out. Setting out the design on 2×4s may help to prevent this, but we decided simply to sacrifice the bottom layer and keep it as our permanent template for the wall.

3. Firewood is usually cut into wedges. Alternate flat sides down with angled edges down to create a stable base.

4. Continue building the wall, using smaller pieces of firewood as infill to give the wall added stability. A good firewood pile should actually have air space between the individual pieces so that the wood can dry and cure properly for burning. Being able to see through your woodpile is the sign of a job well done.

MAPLE SYRUP BUCKET STORAGE

MATERIALS AND TOOLS

3 galvanized sap buckets

3 small screws (⅜" to ½"
  long) with matching nuts

Drill

Drill bit slightly larger than
  diameter of screws

Permanent pen

Nails or screws to attach
  storage bucket to wall

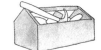 Traditional syrup buckets are simply galvanized buckets that come in a variety of shapes and sizes for different amounts of sap flow. They can be found at gardening and craft stores and can easily be fashioned into handy storage containers for garden gloves, pruners, and the other things that tend to accumulate on your back porch.

1. Lay out buckets in desired pattern. Three in a row work well mounted to a wall. Drill a hole in first bucket where it will meet up with second bucket.

2. Place second bucket in desired position next to first bucket. With a permanent pen, make a mark through hole in first bucket onto second bucket. Drill out second hole.

3. Connect the 2 buckets with the screw and a nut. Hand-tighten.

4. Follow same process with remaining bucket, connecting it to other 2 so that buckets are in a row.

5. Drill a hole in back of each bucket to attach unit to the wall. Drill drainage holes in bottom of buckets, if desired. Attach to wall with nails or screws.

When Becky Wagner from Olga's Cup and Saucer in Providence, Rhode Island, made pizza on an episode of *Cultivating Life*, we knew we had found a kindred spirit. Her passion for making everything herself (from her own ironwork table and chairs to bread racks for housing the bakery's artisanal bread) provides us all with inspiration to take on new things. Meanwhile, her maple scones give us a welcome break from all that we do take on.

CANDIED WALNUTS
½ cup maple syrup
½ cup maple sugar
2 cups walnut pieces

SCONES
9 cups flour
2 teaspoons baking soda
4 teaspoons baking powder
1 teaspoon salt
1 cup maple sugar
1 pound butter
2 cups yogurt
1 cup maple syrup, plus extra
  for brushing tops
1 teaspoon maple extract

1. To make the candied walnuts, bring maple syrup to a boil. Add maple sugar and let boil until sugar dissolves. Add nuts and stir until evenly incorporated. Spread the mixture on a sheet pan lined with parchment paper and let cool. When the candied walnut mixture has cooled, break it up into small pieces. Set aside.

2. Preheat the oven to 400 degrees F. Combine dry ingredients in a large mixing bowl. Add butter and crumble with fingers until the dough takes on the consistency of cornmeal.

3. In a small bowl, mix together yogurt, the 1 cup maple syrup, and maple extract. Add to dry mixture and combine.

4. Add candied walnuts and gently fold into dough. Roll dough out on a cool surface until about ¾ inch thick. Cut with a cookie cutter into your desired shape. Place the scones on a baking tray lined with parchment paper and brush tops with maple syrup.

5. Bake in the oven for about 30 minutes, until tops are golden brown. Rotate the trays midway through to ensure even baking.

MATERIALS

1"×8"×8' oak board

1⅝" ceramic-coated brass
   screws

2 exterior-grade 1" hinges

1 exterior-grade two-piece
   latch

Exterior wood glue

Paint or stain (optional)

TOOLS

Pencil

Table saw

Miter saw

Dado blade

Tape measure

Drill

Screw bit, screw gun, or
   screwdriver

Countersink drill bit

Palm sander

Fine-grade sandpaper

A simple hardwood hanging caddy for small gardening tools such as pruners and trowels prevents having to constantly run back and forth between the shed or garage and the garden. In addition, especially for those of us likely to leave our tools out in the rain, it gives us a place to keep our tools at hand and safe from the elements.

1. Cut out the following pieces from 1"×8" board:
   14½"×7½" (1 piece—back)
   16"×7½" (2 pieces—top and bottom)
   9"×7½" (2 pieces—sides)
   14⅜"×4⅞" (1 piece—front door panel)
   14½"×1½" (1 piece—bottom front face board)

2. Set up dado blade on table saw to ¾" (width of oak stock). Notch out 7½" sides of top and bottom pieces. This will create notch for rabbet joint.

3. To create a 5-degree pitch on top of box to allow for water runoff, take each side piece and mark left side at 8⅞" and right side at 7⅜", connect 2 marks, and cut on this line.

4. Fasten bottom to sides, with each side recessed into notch to create rabbet joint. Predrill holes for screws, countersink holes, apply wood glue to the joints, and fasten with screws. Next, attach back and the bottom front boards to bottom and sides. Both will sit flush inside the bottom and side panels. Fasten in place with both glue and screws. Predrill and countersink holes for screws.

5. Using table saw with a general-purpose blade, take the front door and rip a 45-degree bevel along length of 14⅜" side. This bevel will allow door to open and close freely without being hung up on bottom front face board. Attach door to top with hinges, being sure door sits between 2 notches and with beveled edge facing down and in.

6. Attach top to box, fastening in place with both glue and screws. Predrill and countersink holes for screws.

7. To protect the oak from the elements, sand lightly and apply paint or stain to exterior of box.

8. Finally, attach latch to bottom front face and door and hang unit on wall or fence from inside back using screws.

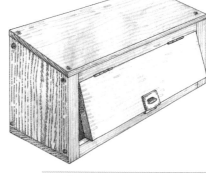

The storage box can be mounted on a wall or a fence

Japanese maples are noted for their widely varied leaf forms and the wonderful colors many varieties take on as the season progresses. Some forms of Japanese maple are dwarf or slow-growing; this makes them ideal choices for growing in containers, because they will not outgrow their pots too quickly. Once you establish them in containers, you can move these handsome specimens around the garden or terrace.

As in the art of bonsai, keeping a tree in a container requires some attention. Because the roots of the tree will eventually outgrow the container, it is best to root-prune the tree annually (once it has started to fill the container) to maintain the plant's size and to ensure the vigor of the root system. Simply remove the plant from the container and trim back the roots by about a quarter, scoring the sides of the root ball to promote new outward-facing growth. At the same time, replenish the surrounding soil with fresh potting mix.

Never use topsoil for potting a tree because it will compact in the container and cut off much-needed air circulation to the roots of the tree. Instead, use a well-balanced soilless potting medium.

Cultivating Life contributor Cynthia Treen shared with us a simple way to capture the beauty of falling leaves for posterity with these hanging leaf sculptures. A series of them hung on a wall makes a wonderful kinetic sculpture. If you have friends who live in Southern California, Florida, or Hawaii, it makes a great gift, giving them a glimpse of the beauty of fall.

MATERIALS AND TOOLS

Mat knife
One ¼"×½"×24" length of basswood (available at art and architectural supply stores)
Fine sandpaper
Clean, dried leaf
One ½" brass weight with loop (see Resources)
10" of .015" piano wire (available at art and architectural supply stores)
Drill
¹⁄₁₆" bit
Small upholstery tacks or brads
Quick-drying, permanent adhesive, such as Krazy Glue
Hammer

1. Using mat knife, cut a 1" length from basswood. Sand edges with fine-grade sandpaper on a 45-degree angle to create a beveled edge on 4 sides of front of basswood.

2. Drill a hole ¾" deep through center of the top of thin short side of basswood.

3. Drill a hole through beveled front panel slightly in from all 4 corners. These holes are for brads that will attach the sculpture to the wall.

4. Fold one end of piano wire so that the last ½" forms a hook. Bend wire into a soft arc and set aside. (Running 2 fingers along wire on top and bottom should create arc easily.)

5. Glue flat side of leaf to brass weight and set aside to dry.

6. Place straight end of wire into hole on top of basswood piece so that the wire arcs downward. Glue into place so that the wire hangs directly in front of basswood base. Allow to dry.

7. Using small brads or furniture tacks and a hammer, attach wood base to wall where it will hang.

8. Hang the weighted leaf from hook on end of wire through loop on brass weight.

COMPOST BIN

MATERIALS

One 2"×4"×8' cedar board
Three 2"×4"×10' cedar boards
Four 2"×4"×12' cedar boards
Two 1"×6"×10' cedar boards
Four 1"×5"×12' cedar boards
2½" and 1½" stainless steel
    screws
26'×36"×½" galvanized
    hardware cloth
¾" galvanized poultry staples
Twelve 4"×⅜" galvanized
    carriage bolts with
    matching washers and
    nuts
Exterior wood glue

TOOLS

Pencil
Hammer
Adjustable wrench
Miter saw
Table saw
Dado blade
Drill
Screw bit, screw gun, or
    screwdriver
⅜" wood paddle bit
Tape measure
Countersink drill bit
Plug cutter
Pencil
Hammer
Palm sander
Medium-grade sandpaper

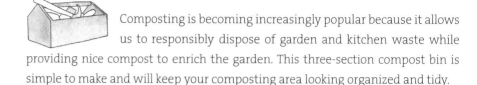

Composting is becoming increasingly popular because it allows us to responsibly dispose of garden and kitchen waste while providing nice compost to enrich the garden. This three-section compost bin is simple to make and will keep your composting area looking organized and tidy.

1. From 2"×4"×10' and 2"×4"×12' stock, cut out:
    Three 9' lengths (from the three 10' lengths)
    Eight 3' lengths (from two 12' lengths)
    Eight 32½' lengths (from two 12' lengths)

2. Construct 4 dividers, which will be 34" tall and 36" wide. The corners will be connected with a rabbet joint for strength. Set up dado blade on the table saw to a height of ¾" and notch out each end of one side of all eight 3' lengths. The notch should be 1½" wide (the width of 32½" boards).

3. Fasten frame of each divider together with exterior wood glue and 2½" stainless steel screws. Countersink the screws visible on front top of each divider so they can be hidden with plugs later.

4. Using hammer, attach galvanized hardware cloth to one side of each divider with poultry staples. Be sure enough staples are used to keep attached to frame, as the compost will be pressing against it.

5. Stand each frame up with 34" side being used as height and space each frame 2'7" apart, making sure countersunk screws are facing downward. For the 2 outer panels, be sure that the side with the hardware cloth is facing in. Attach a 2"×4"×9' to both the front and back of the top of dividers. Use ⅜" paddle bit to predrill the holes and fasten with carriage bolts. Once all 8 carriage bolts are secured, flip unit over. Attach last remaining 2"×4"×9' to back top of dividers with 4 remaining carriage bolts.

6. Attach hardware cloth to the back side of the compost bin with poultry staples. This is done on the back side with one continuous length of hardware cloth.

7. Using table saw, cut four 35½" lengths from 1×6 cedar. Rip down 2 of these boards to a width of 4½". Attach 2 wider boards to 2 center dividers. Be sure 1×6 is centered on 2×4 divider frame so that the edges of the 1×6 overhang the 2×4 equally on both sides. These overhangs will act as one side of pockets used to hold removable front panels. Use countersink drill bit and 1½" stainless steel screws to fasten these boards to dividers at top and bottom.

8. Attach 2 narrower width boards to end dividers with overhang running only along side closest to interior of bin. Use countersink drill bit and 1½" stainless steel screws to fasten these boards to dividers.

9. Rip down remaining 2×4 stock into six 1"×1"×34" pieces to create back sides of pockets. Attach to divider frame with 1½" stainless steel screws so they are set 1" back from front side of pockets. This will create a slot into which front panels can be inserted.

10. With remaining 1×6 stock, cut out 18 front panels at an approximate length of 2'6½". (These panels may need to be fit to size, after bin is fully constructed.) Once cut to appropriate length, sand each end edge of panels to prevent chipping and so that panels will slide more smoothly into pockets.

Removable front panels slide in and out of overhangs between dividers

Planting and Pruning a Copper Beech Hedge
(page 240)

NOTE

The trees can be balled and burlapped, bare root (if available), or containerized. Although containerized trees will be the easiest to plant, bare-root trees ordered from a nursery for planting early in the season would be the most economical.

It's hard to complain about a neighbor who provides a carefully clipped wall of green instead of the backside of a fence. And, though there is some maintenance in terms of pruning and care, it is more fun to clip a hedge than to paint a fence. Plus, how many fences provide a nesting place for songbirds? So perhaps it isn't good fences that make great neighbors but good hedges.

With a little work, a clipped hedge can provide stylish privacy and a living fence for many years. Hedges also make a wonderful backdrop for perennial gardens, helping to highlight plantings by creating a wall of green (or purple if one uses copper beeches) against which perennials show off their true colors.

When most people think of hedges, they think shrubs. But some trees can make a spectacular hedge because they can be pruned hard and kept at a reasonable height. · *Photograph on page 238*

PLANTING A HEDGE

1. Select trees with nice straight trunks. Beeches and hornbeams are most commonly used for this sort of hedge. If considering another type of tree, ask at your local nursery whether it will take to the regular pruning that these hedges require.

2. Select your site and prepare it for planting. Amend the soil with compost and dig a trench as deep as the rootball of the trees and twice as wide. For bare-root trees, prepare the soil and set each tree in place with the roots positioned to spread out over a mound of soil in planting hole so that the place where the roots meet the trunk of the tree is level with the soil line or slightly above. Planting a tree too deeply can undermine its chance of survival.

3. Plant trees in a line about 3 feet apart and make sure the trunks are perfectly aligned with one another by using a guideline attached to two poles on the ends of the hedge. Water in and let the trees settle in for their first year.

PRUNING IN SUBSEQUENT YEARS

1. Set up a guideline so trees can be pruned in a perfect line. Tree hedges are meant to be very formal and really precise. With pruning shears and loppers, cut back any branches that go past the guideline.

2. In the first year after planting, cut the branches back by about two-thirds of their length. It will seem drastic, but the tree will recover and this will ensure a thick hedge. Cutting back branches will cause the tree's growth to thicken, as every cut will be replaced not by one branch but two. Trees can be pruned several times a year to create a formal hedge. If properly maintained, they can be kept as narrow as 18 inches to 2 feet in depth.

Many people are fascinated by these upright so-called cornbeams. These trees are actually a columnar or fastigiate form of hornbeam *(Carpinus)* and received their cornbeam moniker from a friend who misheard the tree's common name.

To create a similar effect, plant a straight-trunked hornbeam (fastigiate beech also work for this process) and trim it back deeply each year to create a series of tightly held branches. As the tree develops, it can be trained into this form, using hand shears or pruners (electric trimmers tend to shred the branches). It may require multiple prunings in a year.

At his home in the Netherlands, our friend Piet Oudulf has created this effect with silver weeping pears that he has trained in a rectangular form, which is equally appealing and takes a more straightforward pruning. The principles are the same as creating a clipped hedge (see opposite).

acknowledgments

Bringing a book to fruition requires the help and support of many people. The team of people who helped make this book a reality was filled with the creativity that made the book into all that it is.

We are greatly indebted to our photographer for the project, Webb Chappell, as well as those who helped fill his beautiful shots with inspiring ideas, recipes, and projects. Cynthia Treen, Wes Martin, Mike Hutchison, Brian Birch, Matthew Gleason, Eric Pilotte, Sandra King, Jacquie Borden, Scott Olnhausen, and Tovah Martin helped us to pull all of the details of the book together—all while keeping our spirits up during long, hot summer shoots—in ways for which we will always be grateful. Other friends, such as Nancy Hemenway, Mark Sottnick and Doris Wilhouski, Kyle Kelly, Matt Gennuso, Stan and Anya Wallach, Gilberto Nobrega, Keith McManus, Aliza Green, Peter Wooster, and Patricia Chappell, kindly shared their ideas, vision, and homes to fill these pages.

We would also like to thank our publishers, who went beyond the call of duty in turning this project into a book that we can be proud of. Publisher Ann Bramson provided advice and experience. Editor Trent Duffy brilliantly oversaw the editorial direction of the book and kept things rolling along, while production editor Sigi Nacson watched over our grammar and ensured that our directions were as clear as possible, and Erin Sainz assisted with all things administrative. Stephanie Huntwork and Jan Derevjanik worked hard to design a book that made all of the work worthwhile. Nancy Murray assured that this book was beautifully produced. Our publicist, Amy Corley, shared her ideas for promoting the book. On the other side of the publishing fence, our agent, Charlotte Sheedy, has been a true friend and a cheerleader who makes one understand all that an agent can be.

—SEAN CONWAY AND LEE ALAN BUTTALA

I would also like to thank my many friends and team members at Target Corporation with whom I have had the great fortune to work with, learn from, and laugh with. Michael Francis, John Pellegrene, Gail Dorn, Bob Ulrich, Greg Duppler, Laura Hawkins, Chad Bogdan, JoEllen Preradovic, LeeAnn Stevens, Mike Fischer, John Butcher, and Karen Gershman are but a few of the talented Target team members who have helped to realize my dream of bringing a brand to life.

Special thanks to Bette Midler for her kind words and to Roberta Greene for all her help.

Fortunately, I had the good sense to marry my wife, Liz, without whose support none of this would have been possible—thank you, Liz. To my children, Emmett and Fiona, who have to put up with me every day, thanks for being the incredible kids you are. I would also like to thank my mother and father for always telling me I could do anything I wanted in life, and if I did what I loved to the best of my ability, I would always be successful.

—SEAN CONWAY

When we first started creating the television show *Cultivating Life,* the ideas for what the show would be were constantly in flux. Sean and I both knew that we loved to garden and be outdoors, but we didn't want to create a standard garden show, because horticulture was connected to our lives and the lives of those around us in a different manner. It wasn't about just planting perennials in groups of threes, fives, and sevens; what really resonated with us was exploring the outdoors and our relationship to the natural world.

My thanks need to begin with the people who gave me that connection. My family saw the world through the same prism with which we saw everything in producing the show and this book. Whether it's memories of my father checking on his prized tomatoes—hybrid beefsteaks were all the rage in the sixties and seventies and still have a place in the garden—at the end of a long workday (with a pen knife and a salt shaker in tow for emergency tastings); of harvesting fruit at our cottage that my mother then turned into jams and preserves; or of sitting in the backyard and peeling peaches that were then dropped into Chianti for a seasonal take on sangria to be shared with whoever was coming over that night, it is my parents whom I owe for my connection to the land. For me, this book truly belongs to the family, friends, coworkers, and neighbors who shared their ideas, not for the creation of a book, but for the purpose of a better life.

I would also like to thank my dear friend Claire Shaffner for her beach house in Charleston—an inspiring place to finish the final pages of the manuscript during my family's annual vacation (a moment when I was decidedly not cultivating life to its fullest but for which my family was very understanding). While I was locked away writing, the screams of delight emanating from the pool from Jake, Emma, Jackson, Anna, and Bridgette provided inspiration for passing on the love of outdoor living to the next generation of our family.

And lastly, I thank my partner, Gary Christensen, for his support—both technical and emotional—in getting this book off the ground. Over the past eleven years of building stone retaining walls, planting borders, and whatever home improvement project has currently overtaken us, he has kept me sane and helped me to see the value of our hard work, and for this I am grateful. To paraphrase a line of his, I know that I should never buy a lottery ticket because on the day I met him I used up all of the luck allotted to anyone for a lifetime.

Without friends and family, the seed of this idea would never have begun to germinate.

—LEE BUTTALA

resources

BASSWOOD STICKS
MisterArt
800-721-0315
www.misterart.com

BRASS WEIGHTS STYLE, #: BR7384
www.metalliferous.com

GLASS MULCH FOR AGAVES
American Specialty Glass
829 North 400 West
North Salt Lake, UT 84054
801-294-4222
www.americanspecialty-
   glass.com

LEAF SCULPTURE
Spring steel piano wire
   (available from architectural supply stores)
Special Shapes Co.
800-51-shape
www.specialshapes.com

MINIATURE ORCHIDS
J and L Orchids
20 Sherwood Road
Easton, CT 06612
www.jlorchids.com

SPROUTING SEEDS
The Sprout People
887-777-6887
www.sproutpeople.com

SUN PRINT PAPER AND FABRIC
Blue Sunprints
800-894-9410
www.bluesunprints.com

index

NOTE: Page numbers in *italics* refer to illustrations.

A-frames, for tomatoes, *58*, 59–60, *59*
agaves with glass mulch, 109, *109*
apple basket lamp, 212–13, *213*
armoire, chicken wire, *51*
asparagus, planting, 40–41
Atkins, Anna, 53

bamboo fountain, 192–93, *192*
bamboo place mats, 54, *54*
bamboo trellis, 110–11, *110*, *111*
Banks, Joseph, 112
basil, freezing, 81
basket, weed, *211*
basket lamp, apple, 212–13, *213*
bat house, mushroom wood, 154–55, *155*
Bean Curry with Cauliflower, 24, *24*
bean towers, *20*, 22–23, *23*
bean trellis, 26–27, *26*, *27*
bean votives, *29*
begonias, propagating, *105*
Belgian fence, *204*, 206–7, *207*
Bench(es):
    lath, *96*, 98–99
    orchard ladder plant stand, *208*, 209–10
    pine, 168–69, *169*
birdbath for marginal plants, 184, *184*
bird feeder for sunflower seed, *140*, 142–43
birdhouse(s):
    owl house, 146–47, *147*
    saltbox, 144–45, *144*

bog container garden, *182*, 183, *183*
bucket, maple syrup, storage, 230, *230*
building your own projects, 35
    dado blade, *60*
    rabbet joint, *38*
bulbs, 195–203
    drying, curing, braiding, 198–99, *198*
    onion basket planter, *201*
    onionskin eggs, 203, *203*
    outdoor forcing, 196–97, *196*
    rain lilies, *187*
    storing dahlias, 202, *202*
butterfly observation cage, *148*, 151
butterfly pillow, *152*, 153
butterfly plants, 150

candles:
    bean votives, *29*
    milk glass luminarias, *171*
    rice paper votives, 139, *139*
    squash luminaria, *218*
cannas, storing, 202, *202*
cast-iron hanging herb garden, 74, 76, *76*
Cauliflower and Pumpkin Gratin, 221, *221*
cedar orchid box, 102–3, *102*
cedar potting bench, *36*, 37–39
chicken wire armoire, *51*
children's porch swing, *160*, 161–62, *162*
Chile Ristras, 72–73
chimney pots, terra-cotta, *177*

citrus, growing in containers, 125, *125*

clothesline trellis, *172*, 173–74, *174*

coatrack, faucet handle, 190, *191*

cold frame, *32*, 33–34

Community Supported Agriculture (CSA), 25

compost bin, 236–37, *236*, *237*

conifers, dwarf, 92

containerized water gardens, 180–81, *181*

container(s):

    bog garden, *182*, 183, *183*

    growing citrus in, 125, *125*

    Japanese maples in, 234, *234*

copper beech hedge, planting and pruning, 240

cork-lined frame, 129, *129*

corncrib storage, *66*, 67–69, *69*

Cornell, Joseph, 16

cornhusk labels, *71*

corn printing, 65, *65*

Cozzens, Suzi, 138

dado blade, *60*

dahlias, storing, 202, *202*

doghouse, setting up and customizing, *156*, 158–59

dwarf conifers, 92

edging, stone, *95*

eggs, onionskin, 203, *203*

English Beer Mustard, 131

epiphytic plants, 101, 116, *117*

espaliers, 206–7

faucet handle coatrack, 190, *191*

fauna, 141–55

    bat house, mushroom bat, 154–55, *155*

    butterfly observation cage, *148*, 151

    butterfly pillow, *152*, 153

    butterfly plants, 150

    owl house, 146–47, *147*

    saltbox birdhouse, 144–45, *144*

    sunflower seed bird feeder, *140*, 142–43

fence, Belgian, *204*, 206–7, *207*

ferns, 1

    Fiddlehead, Salad, 3, *3*

    green roof for shed, *4*, 5–6

    onion basket planter, *201*

    printing, 65

    propagating, 8–9

    stand, *xviii*, 2

    tree, for mounting miniature orchids, *100*, 101

    under glass, *10*

    vase, fern, 7, *7*

Feta Cheese and Watermelon Salad with Raspberry Vinaigrette, *118*, 120

Fiddlehead Fern Salad, 3, *3*

flora, 97–117

    agaves with glass mulch, 109, *109*

    bamboo trellis, 110–11, *110*, *111*

    butterfly plants, 150

    cedar orchid box, 102–3, *102*

    climbing rose trellis, *106*, 107–8, *108*

    epiphytic, 101, 116, *117*

    herbarium specimens, 112–13, *112*

    lath bench for, *96*, 98–99

    marginals, 184

    mounting miniature orchids, *100*, 101

    poison ivy prints, 114–15, *115*

    propagating begonias, *105*

    rain lilies, *187*

    rose cuttings, 104, *104*

    storing dahlias, 202, *202*

    tillandsia mobile, 116–17, *117*

forcing bulbs, 196–97, *196*

fountain, bamboo, 192–93, *192*

frame, cork-lined, 129, *129*

fruit, 119–25

    Feta Cheese and Watermelon Salad with Raspberry Vinaigrette, *118*, 120

    growing citrus in containers, 125, *125*

    orangery planter, *122*, 123–24

    Small-Batch Preserves, 120, *121*

garlic:
    drying, curing, braiding, 198–99, *198*
    planting, 198
    soft-neck and stiff-neck, 198
    topping and tailing, 199
gilding a lily pad table, 185, *185, 186*
glass, ferns under, *10*
glass mulch, agaves with, 109, *109*
gourd lamp, 216, *217*
Grainy White Wine and Honey Herb Mustard,
    131

hanging box, cedar, for orchids, 102–3, *102*
hanging kitchen gardens, 64, *64, 74, 76, 76*
harvest, 205–21
    apple basket lamp, 212–13, *213*
    Belgian fence, *204,* 206–7, *207*
    gourd lamp, 216, *217*
    heirloom pumpkins, 220, *220*
    lightbulb strings, *214,* 215
    orchard ladder plant stand, *208,* 209–10
    squash luminaria, *218*
    weed basket, *211*
hedge(s):
    copper beech, planting and pruning, *238,*
        240
    stilted or pleached, topiary, 175, *175*
heirloom pumpkins, saving seeds of, 220, *220*
heirloom tomatoes, saving seeds of, 62, *63*
herbs, 75–81
    backdoor pot, 77, *77*
    cast-iron hanging garden, *74, 76, 76*
    drying, storing, freezing, 81
    herbarium specimens, 112–13, *112*
    rail planter, *78,* 79–80, *79*
Herman, Robert, 5
home, 157–77
    children's porch swing, *160,* 161–62, *162*
    clothesline trellis, *172,* 173–74, *174*
    doghouse, *156,* 158–59
    fixing terra-cotta pots, 176, *176*
    iron fence table, 163, *163*

milk glass luminarias, *171*
milk-painted stools, 170, *170*
pine bench, 168–69, *169*
screen door curtain, 164–65, *165*
stilted hedge topiary, 175, *175*
stock shed, *167*
terra-cotta chimney pots, *177*
hornbeams, pruning, 241, *241*
horseradish, planting, 41
hypertufa:
    nursery pots, *91,* 93
    troughs, 92, 94

iron fence table, 163, *163*

Japanese maples in containers, 234, *234*
Jefferson, Thomas, ix
Jerusalem artichokes, planting, 41

ladder plant stand, *208,* 209–10
lamp(s):
    apple basket, 212–13, *213*
    gourd, 216, *217*
    sculptural willow, 226, *227*
land art woodpile, *228,* 229
lath bench for houseplants and orchids, *96,*
    98–99
leaf sculpture, 235, *235*
lightbulb strings, *214,* 215
luminaria:
    milk glass, *171*
    squash, *218*
Luth, Old Farmer, x–xi

Maple Scones, 231, *231*
maple syrup bucket storage, 230, *230*
marginal plants, birdbath for, 184, *184*
microgreens, growing, *133,* 134
milk bottle carrier, *55*
milk glass luminarias, *171*
milk-painted stools, 170, *170*
mobile, tillandsia, 116–17, *117*

moss(es):

    mossy pots, *11*

    shadow box, 16, *17*

    spike, *15*

    tropical jars, 15, *15*

mushroom print plates, *18*, 19

mushroom wood bat house, 154–55

mustard, recipes, 131

mustard from seed, 130, *130*

oak storage box, 232–33, *232, 233*

onion basket planter, *201*

onions:

    drying, curing, braiding, 198–99, *198*

    planting, 198

    topping and tailing, 199

onionskin eggs, 203, *203*

orangery planter, *122*, 123–24

orchard ladder plant stand, *208*, 209–10

orchid box, cedar, 102–3, *102*

orchids, miniature, mounting, *100*, 101

Oudulf, Piet, 241

outdoor kitchen, *42*, 43–55, *45*

    bamboo place mats, 54, *54*

    barbecue trug, *47*

    budget, 44

    chicken wire armoire, *51*

    flexibility, 45

    milk bottle bar, 55

    plumbing and electricity, 46

    protecting from the elements,

        45–46

    siting, 44–45

    storage, 46

    sun prints, 52, 53

    tool carriers, *47, 48*, 49, 55

    utensil caddy, oak, *48*, 49

owl house, 146–47, *147*

paper, making, 138, *138*

parsley, freezing, 81

pebble mosaic pots, *88*, 89, *89*

peppers:

    Making Chile Ristras, 72–73, *73*

    oven drying, 72, 73

    roasting and freezing, 73

pillows, butterfly, *152*, 153

pine bench, 168–69, *169*

Pine Nut–Crusted Tomatoes, 61, *61*

Piotte, Eric, 37

place mats, bamboo, 54, *54*

planter(s):

    onion basket, *201*

    orangery, *122*, 123–24

    portable salad table, 30–31, *30, 31*

    herb rail, *78*, 79–80, *79*

    raised seedbed, *126*, 128

    tabletop rice paddy, *136*, 137

planting perennial vegetables, 40–41

plates, mushroom print, *18*, 19

pleached or stilted hedge topiary, 175, *175*

poison ivy prints, 114–15, *115*

porch swing, children's, *160*, 161–62, *162*

portable salad table, 30–31, *30, 31*

pot(s):

    backdoor herb, 77, *77*

    chimney, *177*

    growing citrus in, 125, *125*

    hypertufa, 93

    mossy, *11*

    pebble mosaic, *88*, 89, *89*

    terra-cotta, fixing, 176, *176*

potting bench, cedar, *36*, 37–39

Preserves, Small-Batch, 120, *121*

projects, building your own, 35

pumpkins:

    and Cauliflower Gratin, 221, *221*

    curing, 220

    heirloom, 220, *220*

rabbet joint, *38*

rail planter, herb, *78*, 79–80, *79*

rain barrel, 188, *188*

rain gauge, 189, *189*

rain lilies, *187*

raised seedbed, *126*, 128

recipes:

    Bean Curry with Cauliflower, 24, *24*

    Chile Ristras, 72–73, *73*

    English Beer Mustard, 131

    Feta Cheese and Watermelon Salad with
        Raspberry Vinaigrette, *118*, 120

    Fiddlehead Fern Salad, 3, *3*

    Grainy White Wine and Honey Herb
        Mustard, 131

    Maple Scones, 231, *231*

    Pine Nut–Crusted Tomatoes, 61, *61*

    Pumpkin and Cauliflower Gratin, 221, *221*

    Small-Batch Preserves, 120, *121*

rhubarb, planting, 41

rice paddy, tabletop, *136*, 137

rice paper:

    making, 138, *138*

    votives, 139, *139*

roof, green, for shed, *4*, 5–6

rooting, willow water for, 225

rose cuttings, 104, *104*

roses, climbing, trellis for, *106*, 107–8, *108*

saltbox birdhouse, 144–45, *144*

Scones, Maple, 231, *231*

screen door curtain, 164–65, *165*

sculptural willow lamp, 226, *227*

sculpture, leaf, 235, *235*

seed packet cork frame, 129, *129*

seed(s):

    growing microgreens, *133*, 134

    growing sprouts, *132*, 135

    heirloom pumpkins, 220, *220*

    heirloom tomatoes, 62, *63*

    mustard from, 130, *130*, 131

    raised seedbed, *126*, 128

    storing, 128

    sunflower, bird feeder for, *140*, 142–43

shadow box, 16, *17*

shallots:

    harvesting, drying, curing, 198–99, *198*

    planting, 198

shed:

    green roof for, *4*, 5–6

    stock, *167*

slate-topped side table, 86–87, *86*, *87*

Small-Batch Preserves, 120, *121*

sprouts, growing, *132*, 135

squash:

    and Cauliflower Gratin, 221, *221*

    curing, 220

    heirloom, 220, *220*

    luminaria, *218*

stilted or pleached hedge topiary, 175, *175*

stock shed, *167*

stone, 83–95

    artificial (hypertufa), 92

    edging, *95*

    hypertufa nursery pots, *91*, 93

    large hypertufa troughs, 94

    pebble mosaic pots, *88*, 89, *89*

    planting troughs with dwarf conifers,
        90, 92

    slate-topped side table, 86–87, *86*, *87*

    tree marker, *82*, 84, *85*

stools, milk-painted, 170, *170*

storage:

    corncrib, *66*, 67–69, *69*

    maple syrup bucket, 230, *230*

    oak box for, 232–33, *232*, *233*

strings, lightbulb, *214*, 215

sunflower seed bird feeder, *140*, 142–43

sun prints, 52, 53

swing, porch, children's, *160*, 161–62, *162*

table(s):

    cedar potting bench, *36*, 37–39

    iron fence, 163, *163*

    lath bench for houseplants and orchids,
        96, 98–99

lily pad, water-gilding, 185, *185, 186*

portable salad, 30–31, *30, 31*

side, slate-topped, 86–87, *86, 87*

terra-cotta chimney pot, *177*

terra-cotta pots, fixing, 176, *176*

tillandsia mobile, 116–17, *117*

tomatoes:

A-frames, *58,* 59–60, *59*

hanging kitchen garden, 64, *64*

heirloom, seeds, 62, *63*

Pine Nut–Crusted, 61, *61*

tool carriers, *47, 48,* 49, *55*

tool holder(s):

maple syrup bucket, 230, *230*

topiary, stilted hedge, 175, *175*

Treen, Cynthia, 235

trees, 223–41

compost bin, 236–37, *236, 237*

copper beech hedge, *238,* 240

dwarf conifers, *90,* 92

espaliers, 206–7

Japanese maples in containers, 234, *234*

land art woodpile, *228,* 229

leaf sculpture, 235, *235*

Maple Scones, 231, *231*

maple syrup bucket storage, 230, *230*

oak storage box, 232–33, *232, 233*

pruning hornbeams, 241, *241*

sculptural willow lamp, 226, *227*

siting, 224

stone marker, *82,* 84, *85*

willow water for rooting, 225

trellis(es):

bamboo, 110–11, *110, 111*

bean, 26–27, *26, 27*

climbing rose, *106,* 107–8, *108*

clothesline, *172,* 173–74, *174*

tomato A-frames, *58,* 59–60, *59*

Trillium, *ix*

troughs, hypertufa, *90,* 91, 92, 94

utensil caddy, oak, *48,* 49

vase, fern, 7, *7, 200*

vegetables, 21–41

bean towers, *20,* 22–23, *23*

bean trellis, 26–27, *26, 27*

bean votives, *29*

cold frame, *32,* 33–34

eating local and organic, 25

perennials, planting, 40–41

planting a salad table, 31

portable salad table, 30–31, *30, 31*

votive(s):

bean, *29*

milk glass, *171*

rice paper, 139, *139*

Wagner, Becky, 231

Wallace, Alfred Russel, 112

Ward, Nathaniel, 13

Wardian cases, planting, *12,* 13–14

water, 179–93

bamboo fountain, 192–93, *192*

birdbath for marginals, 184, *184*

bog container garden, *182, 183, 183*

containerized gardens, 180–81, *181*

faucet handle coatrack, 190, *191*

gilding a lily pad table, 185, *185, 186*

rain barrel, 188, *188*

rain gauge, 189, *189*

rain lilies, *187*

Webb, Marguerite, 101

weed basket, *211*

willow lamp, sculptural, 226, *227*

willow water for rooting, 225

woodpile, land art, *228,* 229